Rhetorics of Reason
and Desire

Noah as a preacher. Manuscript illustration. Foto Biblioteca Vaticana
(Vat. Lat. 5409, f. 54r).

Rhetorics of Reason and Desire

VERGIL, AUGUSTINE, AND
THE TROUBADOURS

SARAH SPENCE

Cornell University Press

ITHACA AND LONDON

First published 1988 by Cornell University Press.

International Standard Book Number 0-8014-2129-2
Library of Congress Catalog Card Number 87-47953

Printed in the United States of America

*Librarians: Library of Congress cataloging information
appears on the last page of the book.*

*The paper in this book is acid-free and meets the guidelines for
permanence and durability of the Committee on Production Guidelines
for Book Longevity of the Council on Library Resources.*

For Jim
So near and yet so phare

It is not something that can be put into words like other branches of learning; only after long partnership in a common life devoted to this very thing does truth flash upon the soul, like a flame kindled by a leaping spark.

PLATO, *The Seventh Letter*

Although I can lift my finger to point something out, I cannot supply the vision by means of which either this gesture or what it indicates can be seen.

AUGUSTINE, *De doctrina christiana*

CONTENTS

Illustrations   XI
Preface   XIII
Abbreviations   XVII
Introduction: Desire and the Rhetorical Tradition   I

PART ONE   *The Rhetoric of Cupidity*
1 Vergil's Orator   11
2 Juno's Desire   22

PART TWO   *The Hermeneutics of Charity*
3 Augustine and the Reincorporation of Desire   55
4 Rhetorical Anxiety in Troubadour Lyric   103

Conclusion: Legacy of the Divine Spark   128
Notes   131
Index   153

Illustrations

Noah as a preacher (Vat. Lat. 5409, f. 54r)   FRONTISPIECE

1. Poor posture and good posture   4

2. Adam, Eve, and the paralytic (Mag D 37)   63

3. Orans and the story of Jonah (Lau E 3)   66

4. Veiled orans (Pri L 5)   71

5. Three boys in the furnace with raven (Pri L 12)   74

6. Three boys in the furnace with hand of God (Mag D 25)   75

7. Gabriel appearing to Mary (Pri E 30)   81

8. Moses on Mount Sinai (Din A 3)   91

The frontispiece illustration appears courtesy of the Biblioteca Vaticana; the catacomb photographs are reproduced courtesy of the Pontificia Commissione di Archeologia Sacra, Rome.

PREFACE

Literature and rhetoric are often mentioned in the same context. Both deal in language, with speaker and audience; both aim to persuade. Most often the contact between the two is one of application, rhetoric being used to analyze a given author's figures of speech or style. Yet rhetoric, at least in the Western tradition, is also a guide to culture, to the very culture that produced the literature and its author, and rhetorical treatises often articulate the priorities and values that may inform a literary text even though they remain, for whatever reason, unspoken.

When a literary text deliberately calls upon rhetoric—by modeling its hero on an orator, for example—the relationship between the two becomes more complex. By foregrounding rhetoric an author highlights the ideological framework of the text and, consequently, opens it up to analysis. Such is the case with the texts analyzed here: Vergil offers us the Isocratean orator as model for his hero Aeneas. Augustine explicitly rejects this model in his *Confessions*, replacing it with a revised, Christian rhetor. The troubadours try to return in part to the humanist model without entirely losing the benefits gained by Augustine's revisions.

Each text's reliance on rhetoric and its contextualization seems to extend even further. Vergil suggests a parallel between Aeneas and Isocrates that questions priorities expressed in the humanist rhetorical tradition, such as the valuation of speaker over audience and reason over desire. Augustine continues this quest in his attempt to develop and articulate what is new about Christian thought, and, in so doing, he responds to many of Vergil's implied wishes. The Christian *orans*, as depicted in catacomb paintings and explored in Augustine's writings, is in dialogue with his audience—in mutual deferral to a higher power—and aims to persuade through a combination of reason and desire. Truth is not communicated through language to an audience; rather, it is discovered silently in the hearts of those who ask. By reintroducing desire into rhetorical strategy Augustine opens up the possibility for articulating a renewed worldview in which balance and mediation, not power and oppression, are guiding principles. The troubadours (especially those focused on here: Guilhem IX, Raimbaut d'Aurenga, and Jaufre Rudel) demonstrate their alliance to these Augustinian innovations in their emphasis on desire, but they also lament the concomitant loss of power and control built into this revised rhetoric and point ultimately to its failure when applied in a secular context.

The central issue throughout is desire. Desire entices and lures, and ultimately threatens to undo the very basis of a culture grounded in language and reason, precisely because it can communicate and persuade in ways that cannot be captured by language, that do not follow the predictable laws of reason. Desire's powers are isolating, however, in their emphasis on the single will; they lack the reassurance of community and control.

I am grateful to the American Academy in Rome for awarding me a Rome Prize in Post-Classical Humanistic Studies with which I could begin the research for this work; to California State University, Long Beach, for release time and

summer support; and to the Mellon Faculty Fellowship Program at Harvard University for a year of research and writing.
I also thank Father Umberto Fasola of the Pontificia Commissione di Archeologia Sacra and the Benedettine di Priscilla for enabling me to visit and photograph many Roman catacombs otherwise closed to the public.

Many friends—who may also have been teachers, students, or colleagues—deserve thanks for their contributions to this work. I particularly acknowledge the three students in my freshman seminar at Harvard: Eric Jaso, Matthew Mellen, and, above all, Jessica Riskin (Jessie is due additional thanks for her valiant efforts as my research assistant during the summer that followed); my colleagues and students at California State University, Long Beach, especially those in my seminar on Vergil and Augustine; and Kyle Phillips, Joan Ferrante, and Richard Brilliant for their help at crucial moments.

Bernhard Kendler of Cornell University Press took an early interest in the work and offered helpful suggestions along the way. I am indebted to Robert W. Hanning of Columbia University and Michael C. J. Putnam of Brown University, who read the work in an earlier form, and the readers provided by Cornell University Press, for their constructive criticisms. I also thank Ernie Torres of Long Beach for his work on the manuscript; R. Neil Beshers for his expert copyediting; and Elizabeth Parry for constructing the index.

And, finally, this book would not exist—conceptually or materially—without the three who taught me to read Vergil: Michael Putnam, Helen Bacon, and the late Steele Commager; without its dedicatee, who has done everything he knows (to paraphrase Linda Ronstadt) to show me what Plato meant; and without my parents, whom the book is really about anyway.

SARAH SPENCE

Long Beach, California

ABBREVIATIONS

AJP	*American Journal of Philology*
Atti	*Atti del Congresso internazionale di archeologia cristiana*
AugStud	*Augustinian Studies*
CB	*Classical Bulletin*
CJ	*Classical Journal*
CQ	*Classical Quarterly*
CW	*Classical Weekly/Classical World*
G&R	*Greece and Rome*
RAC	*Rivista di Archeologia Cristiana*
RevEtAug	*Revue des Etudes Augustiniennes*
TAPA	*American Philological Association: Transactions and Proceedings*

Rhetorics of Reason
and Desire

Introduction: Desire and the Rhetorical Tradition

When rhetoric becomes an explicit theme of a literary work the reasons are seldom literary or rhetorical but, instead, ideological. A text in which a major character is compared to an orator belongs to a particular category of works, a subgenre of the literary canon defined by a social and cultural purpose: heroes are not orators unless one of the author's aims is to confront and question the cultural underpinnings of his time. I propose here to look at three such works, broadly understood: Vergil's *Aeneid,* Augustine's *Confessions,* and the lyrics of the troubadours. My aim will be to determine the use these authors make of their respective rhetorical traditions.

All rhetoric, be it humanist or Christian, is concerned ultimately with defining the values of its culture. All Latin definitions of classical rhetoric include the word *bene.* That *bene* is neither gratuitous nor loosely applied; the rhetorical tradition spells out a moral code that reflects a systematic hierarchy of good and bad, right and wrong.

But more, a rhetorical system provides an index to a culture's views on one particular moral issue: the relation of reason to desire and the relative value of reasoning and seduction. A study of rhetoric, or of literature that alludes to a rhetorical system, is always also a study of reason and desire and of how the two interact. Yet it is rarely approached that way; Chaim Perelman and P. Olbrechts-Tyteca's, *The New Rhetoric: A Treatise on Argumentation* comes close to addressing these issues, but even it stops short. More often, the treatises that imitate and study the rhetorical tradition assume a positivistic approach, accepting without question the hierarchies and values asserted by the tradition. George A. Kennedy, in his monumental series of works on classical rhetoric, acknowledges the centrality of rhetoric to classical culture, yet he rarely confronts the values of such a system. By examining both rhetorical treatises and literary works that allude to the centrality of rhetoric, we come quickly to an understanding of how the two faculties of reason and desire interact. In the classical tradition, for instance, reason is celebrated, seduction denigrated. The very necessity to assert such a hierarchy, however, argues loudly for the defining role desire must play in this culture, as the process of hierarchy demands the presence of a rejected, even suppressed figure.

It has been suggested that rhetoric both establishes and articulates the ideals of a culture. It is also true, however, that rhetoric offers a chart of the interaction of those ideals. That is, rhetoric outlines the primary power relationships of a culture. It tells us not only the goals of the culture and their paradigmatic arrangement but also how they interact: what is the basis of power and how that power is used. A rhetoric tacitly defines the reigning dynamics of central power relationships and the role that language and desire will play in their interaction.

Such a definition of rhetoric is not limited to ancient times. All works that refer to a rhetorical system codify through their assertions the dynamics and expectations of even the most private relationships as they explore the ideals of a culture from large to small. For example, in 1933, Olive Richards Landers published a *Hand Book for the Modern Girl*. This work defined its purpose as "starting you going, helping you to find yourself" (p. 1), by teaching young women about such things as personal problems, looks, clothes, and etiquette, to mention only the subjects of the first four chapters. Ostensibly a book of manners, the handbook is also a cultural guide, as morality and ideals are inscribed on every page.

In the chapter on looks Landers includes a drawing (see Figure 1). The caption states that it is an illustration of poor posture and good posture "in walking and standing." Clearly, however, the drawing entails more than posture in its message. The woman on the left—the one with "poor" posture—is outlined by the young tree in the background: the arch of the branches echoes the curve of her spine and the overall configuration of her posture. The woman on the right, however, contrasted with a similar tree, is compared to both the lopped-off tree in the middle ground and the pickets of the fence behind her. Poor posture is thus allied, implicitly, with untamed nature, while good posture is connected either with truncated trees or with manmade objects of containment, like wooden fences.

The illustration suggests further distinctions, however, as the woman with "poor" posture is shown with fashionably high heels and a low-cut neckline, while the woman with "better" form wears flat walking shoes, a double-breasted jacket, and a tie. While both are wearing skirts, the one on the right is dressed to the greatest degree possible like a man, and the values associated with a difference in posture are connected as well with a difference in gender: good refers not only to upright posture but also to the masculine, while poor is associated with the feminine. By dressing the good woman like a man Landers is, I would suggest, establishing her priorities: man is to woman as good is to bad. In the section on clothes she expands this concept as she describes what constitutes proper attire: "We should wear our clothes," she says, "as the bird wears its feathers . . . unconscious of them, as if they had become part of ourselves" (p. 48). Clothes for her are a camouflage that makes difference and seduction disappear. Things like "slippery shoulder straps" and "stray wisps of

1. Poor posture and good posture. From Olive Richards Landers, *Hand Book for the Modern Girl* (Garden City, N.Y.: Greenberg, 1933), p.24.

hair" are condemned; Landers prefers the more genderless costume: "No dress . . . should impede free, graceful movement. . . . This . . . largely accounts for the popularity of the pajama costume" (p. 54). So, too, she instructs her audience to "lower the voice. Every time you hear yourself speaking shrilly, force yourself to repeat what you have said in a lower tone. Even if angry, keep your voice at a low pitch; it will help you get rid of the anger or make you more impressive in it" (p. 41). Like the outfit associated with good posture in the illustration above, the better voice is the lower, more masculine one. She tells her readers to "concentrate on the effect [they] want"; the effect she wants, in her attempt to reduce the presence of desire, is for her audience to associate the good with the upright, civilized, and genderless.

In describing the action of the modern girl, Landers outlines as well the dynamics of an ideal paradigm. Desire is denied, and the action of denial sets in motion the choices of an entire morality. What Landers prescribes is not just a static system but a system as it functions: reason is the faculty equated with what is good, and reasoning the process that keeps the hierarchy intact. The primary relationship of author to audience is similarly construed: the author is allied with the positive and powerful force of reason, while the audience, in its unknown and ultimately enigmatic capacity, is linked with desire.

Such a relation between reason and desire, however popular and familiar, reflects only one perspective. There are other ways in which these two forces can interact, and other rhetorics exist to articulate the different pairings. While Lander's treatise reflects in many ways the priorities of the classical humanist tradition of rhetoric, which begins essentially with Isocrates, there is a competing rhetoric, which really begins with Plato, that reflects different values and priorities. This alternative rhetoric is further developed by the Early Christians: from the writings of the early Fathers and the paintings in the Roman catacombs one can extract a model in which the relationship between speaker and audience had shifted drastically. Organic, not intellectual, this other rhetoric requires the audience to participate. This relational shift reflects a moral shift as well. In these early works and later in the codifying works of Saint Augustine, one finds that reason has been joined by desire: persuasion, Augustine argues, occurs through the balancing of reason and desire, not, as the humanists assert, in desire's suppression. What is newest about this rhetoric, however, is not that desire has been valorized in the rhetorical and moral system but that desire has replaced reason as the organizing force of that system. Desire, rather than reason alone, now governs the shape of rhetoric, and desire provides the force for bonding formerly antagonistic pairs.

Literature that uses a rhetorical framework—whose protagonists are modeled on orators—reflects a culture's rhetoric and morals in the values upheld by the hero; in his relationships, priorities, and choices; and in the very genre in which he appears. Vergil's Aeneas, modeled on the humanist orator, is the hero of a political epic; Augustine's quasi-autobiographical persona in the *Confessions* is the hero of an internalized narrative, an epic in lyric voice; and the troubadours, seemingly as private and autobiographical as Augustine, are also public and political in their performance. Each orator-hero in his genre and his plot represents the rhetorical underpinnings of his author's world.

Yet by assuming a rhetorical model the author—or at least authors as good as Vergil, Augustine, and the troubadours— sets out to contextualize his culture's values. Aeneas is likened to a classical orator so that Vergil can question the choices his hero makes, Augustine serves as codifier of the Christian revolution, borrowing from verbal and visual works of the eras that preceded his, yet his conversion story is also that of an entire culture whose priorities were changing. The troubadours reflect their inheritance of the Augustinian perspective in both their lyric genre and their emphasis on desire, even as they question the amount of control and power left them in their role as performance poets.

The vertical hierarchy of classical rhetoric is replaced by the horizontal balance of Christian; the rejection and suppression of desire are replaced by its inclusion and validation, and the forces that bond the elements together have changed from reason and power to will and faith. As a consequence, the role of language, the orator, and the audience also change: while for Aeneas language is the sole tool necessary for persuasion, for Augustine language is often supplemented by instinct, inspiration, and silence; while Vergil's orator is all-powerful, Augustine's is joined by a participating audience.

From Vergil's presentation of—and disgruntlement with—the perspective of classical rhetoric, then, we move to Augustine's codification of the Christian perspective. From epic we move to inner dialogue. With the troubadours, we move finally to a rejection of Augustinian rhetoric and a call for the humanist return. In each, the orator-hero presents at first the traditional worldview, and the genre chosen also reflects that perspective; as well, however, the use of rhetoric enables the author to question that perspective and to formulate in the literary aspects of his work a new and different view that lies outside the structure of his text. For in its innate ambivalence the literary text, as Julia Kristeva has pointed out, has a capability that treatises lack to call upon more than one paradigm at once. While the assumptions of a given rhetorical model provide a framework for the literary text, within that framework shadowy traces of a would-be worldview can be found.

The texts chosen here are not as isolated as they may first appear: Vergil's problems with his rhetorical system are resolved to a certain degree by Augustine. Augustine's theory creates new problems, which the troubadours confront and question. Put another way, Augustine's response to Vergil's critique of the rhetorical and moral standard establishes a second norm, which proves equally problematical and exclusive, though, at the same time, it allows for a certain restructuring of thought. Troubadour lyric accepts this reorganization as the norm, points to its limitations, and suggests ways in which it needs correction—ways that, I feel, include a partial return to humanism.

It would appear that Augustine's rhetorical model proved less useful as a paradigm than did that of the humanists. While it more than adequately summarized the changes that had occurred in Christian thought during the centuries that preceded his, for future generations it proved largely untenable. As Christianity was rapidly absorbed into the political structure of the empire, it, too, became appropriated by extant hierarchical systems. Yet Augustine's rhetorical model remains important to us for two particular, if unrelated, reasons: first, it helps define and clarify the nature of the medieval text and its audience, and, second, it remains a monument and example of a nonantagonistic approach to persuasion and power. As Landers shows us, the values and priorities the humanists expressed were not unique to them. Desire and its denial are still current issues, as is a paradigm that functions at the expense of the oppressed. Augustine's changes could serve as powerful and valuable lessons for us today.

PART ONE
The Rhetoric of Cupidity

1 VERGIL'S ORATOR

The Rising Hero

In one of the earliest and most memorable scenes from Vergil's *Aeneid*, Neptune rises from the depths of the sea and calms a storm Juno has just caused (*Aen.* 1.124-56). Upset at first ("Quos ego . . .") he quickly regains his composure ("sed motos praestat componere fluctus") and in his calming of the waters occasions the first simile of the epic:

> ac veluti magno in populo cum saepe coorta est
> seditio saevitque animis ignobile vulgus
> iamque faces et saxa volant, furor arma ministrat;
> tum, pietate gravem ac meritis si forte virum quem
> conspexere, silent arrectisque auribus astant;
> ille regit dictis animos et pectora mulcet. (*Aen.* 1.148-53)

As when often in a crowd rebellion is stirred up and the rabble rage in their minds—firebrands and rocks are sent flying and fury provides weapons; then if, by chance, they behold a man, marked by goodness and merit, they fall silent and prick up their ears; and he rules their minds and soothes their souls with words.[1]

More than helping the reader understand Neptune's actions, this simile prepares us, proleptically, for the figure Aeneas cuts when, once landed, he ascends a hill to address and reassure his storm-tossed men (*Aen.* 1.198-207). The simile unites Neptune and Aeneas: in each a man rises to calm an angry and disturbed mob and does so with words alone. The figure presented in the simile is, it is implied, the model that Aeneas, like Neptune, is to be patterned on.

That Aeneas as leader is first characterized this way is, I believe, crucial. It is not, of course, the way in which we first see him: as a nostalgic, almost whimpering figure, wishing he had died on the fields at Troy (*Aen.* 1.92-101); by implicitly comparing both Aeneas as he climbs a hill and Neptune as he rises from the waves to a good man who rules with words, Vergil establishes a paradigm for the ideal and superior figure. This designation is further reinforced by the first depiction of Jupiter (*Aen.* 1.223-96), where words of height and condescension are paired with the calming and persuasive effect of language. A pattern is thus established: all male leaders are described in a similar way and united by means of the first simile of the work.[2]

This thematic, so carefully prepared in the first few pages of the text, is clearly meant to bring to mind a complete set of important associations. The figure in the simile who calms the crowd through language is more than just a peaceful leader. He is an orator, and a representative of one particular branch of that tradition. In carefully designating the model leader as both a good man ("pietate gravem") and one who can calm the irate through language ("regit dictis animos et pectora mulcet"), Vergil calls up the image of the Isocratean orator, the morally good man who demonstrates and improves his ethical integrity by learning to speak persuasively.[3] Good speech, according to Isocrates, is the source of most of our blessings. Although we are inferior to other creatures in most other ways, "there has been implanted in us the power to persuade each other and make clear to each other whatever we desire," and, by virtue of this capacity, we have "escaped the life of wild beasts."[4]

Vergil's simile, in like fashion, suggests that the ideal male—be he mortal or divine—differs from the rabble as man does from beasts: the good man in the simile persuades the angry crowd to be still and prick up its ears ("silent arrectisque auribus astant"); the allusion to the crowd's rabid quality is implicit in this phrase, as is the speaker's ability to change the animal nature through language.

The association between the good man and the orator was developed by Isocrates as an answer to charges that oratory was nothing but chicanery and sophistry. According to Isocrates, the value of oratory is derived from the inherent moral integrity of the speaker and the ability of language to transmit that ethic to the audience. As George A. Kennedy notes, "rhetoric as a system is presumably neither good nor bad; only men are good and bad, and Isocrates would start with a young man who is good." The association between morality and oratory, and between the good man and the orator, remains a "permanent feature of classical rhetoric" and by the time of Vergil has become practically a truism.[5] While Quintilian will later make the most explicit associations of this kind, saying, above all, that the orator must first be a good man (*virum bonum*), Cicero acknowledges a similar adherence to this tradition. In all his prescriptive works Cicero includes such a link between morality and language, as well as an emphasis on the speaker's moral responsibility and superiority over his audience. Clearest perhaps in his earliest, most Aristotelian treatises (such as the *De inventione*), these associations between goodness and oratory, between eloquence and civilization, are never absent from Cicero's works. His definition of rhetoric as *bene dicere* is the one transmitted through the Middle Ages: Cicero's rhetoric, as part of the tradition Isocrates began, is a moral code reflecting a certain system of values.

Vergil's simile, then, has roots in a well-established tradition that associates the best man—the one best suited to lead—with the orator. As we have just glimpsed, however, the tradition from which the simile is drawn involves more than the morality of the speaker and the assertion that the best man will demonstrate his superiority through his speech. Rather, that morality is defined, in both Isocrates and Cicero, by its effect on the audience. Far from being a self-directed goal, the link between good rhetoric and good men includes a notion of community. Isocrates credits eloquence with the founding of the institutions that characterize civilization; Cicero picks up on this concept in his early *De inventione*: in his later *De oratore* that power is translated into the equally public-spirited aims of delighting, teaching, and moving. The orator, in other words, has not fulfilled his obligations by merely being a good man. He must communicate that goodness through his speech and ensure that it have a positive effect on his audience.

Vergil's use of this image includes such a change in his audience. Neptune causes the waves to shift from storm to calm; the man in the simile causes the ignoble rabble to be stilled; Aeneas soothes the anger in himself and his men. In each case, anger, associated with chaos and animal passions, is turned to calm, still, order. This type of transformation likewise has its origin in the rhetorical tradition. Plato's notion of good rhetoric is one that instills order (*Gorgias*); Isocrates' and Cicero's concept that eloquence is a civilizing force suggests as well that good rhetoric is ultimately a process of ordering. Each of these implies that good rhetoric is a rational process. Cicero speaks in the *De inventione* of the pair *oratio-ratio;* the words themselves suggest an innate connection.[6]

In the rhetorical tradition of Isocrates and Cicero to which Vergil alludes in his first simile, the morality that the orator teaches is one in which order and calm are associated, through reason, with the good.[7] Such an association is spelled out most candidly in Cicero's earliest treatise, the *De inventione*, and a look at the relevant passage from that work will help to elucidate further Vergil's first simile.[8]

The Rhetorical Model

The unfinished *De inventione* shares certain assumptions with the rhetorical tradition as a whole.[9] Toward the beginning of this treatise Cicero describes the origins of eloquence. In addition to his echo of Isocrates' claim that rhetoric is a—or perhaps the—generating cultural institution, his founding myth makes clear other interesting *impensées:*

nam fuit quoddam tempus, cum in agris homines passim bestiarum modo vagabantur et sibi victu fero vitam propagabant nec ratione animi quicquam, sed pleraque viribus corporis administrabant, nondum divinae religionis, non humani officii ratio colebatur, nemo nuptias viderat legitimas, non certos quisquam aspexerat liberos, non, ius aequabile quid utilitatis haberet, acceperat. ita propter errorem atque inscientiam caeca ac temeraria dominatrix animi cupiditas ad se explendam viribus corporis abutebatur, perniciosissimis satellitibus. quo tempore quidam magnus videlicet vir et sapiens cognovit, quae materia esset et quanta ad maximas res opportunitas in animis inesset hominum.

For there was a time when men wandered here and there in the fields after the manner of animals, and sustained themselves on wild food; they did not carry out any duties by their rational powers but largely by their physical strength; nor was the institution of worship yet developed, nor of social obligations; no one had yet seen lawful marriage, nor had anyone looked upon children known to be his, nor had he accepted what usefulness just law had. And so, on account of error and ignorance, desire, the blind and reckless mistress of the mind, exploited to its satisfaction physical strength, the most pernicious of henchmen. At this moment, a man, evidently great and wise, learned what materials existed and how much lay in the minds of men to be capitalized upon.[10]

Civilization, Cicero claims, came about because of rhetoric. Chaos was transformed to order by a man who was both wise and eloquent and who could use the tool of reason to organize his fellow men through language; the oratorical capacity gave men superiority over the beasts and the orator power over other humans.[11]

Two important assumptions surface from this etiological tale. First, Cicero sees order as superior to chaos and the orator as the figure who facilitated the change. Second, rhetoric is the primary institution or system of its type: not only is it the first one able to bring the beasts to bay, but Cicero implies that it is also the most important, since it led the way to establishing other cultural and social institutions. Why this is so Cicero also makes clear: not only does eloquence distinguish man from the beasts[12] and the orator from his fellow man,[13] it is also the mark of civilization: in the age before oratory, man did nothing by the guidance of reason. It is the orator who "propter rationem atque orationem" ("by reason and eloquence") introduced all that is useful and civilized.

Cicero's narrative suggests that the transition from chaos to order, and from passion to reason, was absolute—it marked the great divide between the bad times and the good, between then and now. On the grand scale we are on the right side of the divide. But underlying this assertion is a suggestion realized later in the text that the old ways reassert themselves periodically, providing the need for oratory and orators. One implicit rationale for including the etiological tale is, it seems, to provide a model for future orators; not only did the first orator use eloquence to deliver the world from chaos, but every orator is such a person, and every act of oratory, in ritual fashion, redivides chaos from order as it reasserts the superiority of man and reason.[14]

Cicero's understanding of the pragmatics of persuasion reflects his heritage in both Isocratean rhetoric and the Aristotelian tradition of cosmology; his conception of the way persuasion functioned is clearly rooted in Aristotle's understanding of the cosmos. In the *De anima*, man's superiority over the beasts is ascribed to his rational powers; in the *De caelo* and *Physics* this idea is expanded as Aristotle explains that the universe consists of two distinct areas: the sublunar and superlunar.[15] These areas are distinguished by their substance and function: everything beneath the moon is made up of the four elements—earth, water, air, and fire—while everything beyond the moon is made of ether. The elements beneath the moon are interchangeable as long as a due proportion among the elements is retained. Yet none of the four is interchangeable with ether, which, it is implied, is a different substance altogether.[16] Similarly, the four elements beneath the moon are all capable of linear motion, while the objects above the moon move in a circular pattern. Finally, it is the circular movement of the heavens that keeps the sublunary world functioning linearly.[17]

I would suggest that this is a cosmic version of the humanist's attitude toward the role of rhetoric in civilization.[18] To the humanist, chaos and disagreement serve as the defining otherness. Like Aristotle's ether, they must first be clearly identified and labeled, then exiled beyond the immediate area of discussion and there retained as insurance of the separation. The origin of rhetoric was the initial separation of chaos from order, a separation that posited reason as comparable to the physical law of linear motion, which governs the movement of the sublunary world. One may even suggest an analogy between the interchangeability of the four elements and the persuasiveness of mankind. The four elements are interchangeable because they follow the same physical laws: similarly, man can be persuaded from one point of view to another if reason is properly employed. Every good speech begins by identifying the cause of disagreement, then separates the elements that make logical sense—those that can be proved by example or enthymeme—from those that do not. The irrational arguments are thus disposed of, and their irrationality is dwelt upon frequently as a way of ensuring the success of the rational argument, just as the circular motion of the planets ensures the linear motion of the sublunary elements.

I have insisted on this analogy because it seems to correspond to the absolutes that govern the humanist rhetoric alluded to in Vergil's first simile. Neither the humanists nor Aristotle supports the notion of a void; the ineffable is neither physically nor conceptually possible for either of them.[19] Yet the concept of a dump site—be it ether or the opposing side—serves to define through negation the proper and fitting area in which to function. In Aristotle's case that suitable space is the sublunary world, in the humanist's it is the realm of reason.

Humanist rhetoric can be seen, then, as a translation of Aristotle's cosmology into personal terms. It reflects Aristotle's ideas of separation and modal distinction and then charges that distinction with a hierarchical differentiation. Implicit in the humanist's hierarchism is the notion that reason is a force as well as a presence: reasoning, like linear motion, is the proper and appropriate energy, while passion is denied its verb and introduced as only an unwanted presence.

The humanist rhetorical model is also a model of Roman society and culture.[20] It communicates not only the ideals of that world but also the modes of interaction considered appropriate, as it establishes a clear and telling hierarchy that extends beyond the forum and into the most intimate relationships. In establishing the rapport between speaker and audience, rhetorical treatises outline a societal and moral paradigm that communicates the relative merits granted reason and desire in a culture. For Cicero, as for Isocrates and Vergil, the ideal of a civilized human being was the orator, as he was the man best equipped to persuade his audience through rational discourse.[21]

Eloquence, then, is a means by which animals become men, differences are erased, and chaos is transformed to order as the morality of the speaker is communicated and transferred to the audience. Such a process, with its emphasis on morality and virtue, also includes an implicit pattern of choices.[22] The association among eloquence, virtue, and reason, certainly a venerable cluster of qualities, asserts its superiority even as it establishes a clear hierarchy of good and bad, right and wrong.

Vergil's use of the rhetorical simile, which from the start unites both Neptune and Aeneas with the model of the humanist orator, suggests that he meant such a figure to be viewed as the personification of virtue; the priorities of the *Aeneid* seem to be established, even unveiled, in this opening simile. In every rhetorical treatise or definition, however, the definition of such an orator and *magnus vir* is accompanied by a threatening and opposing system of persuasion—one that is often labeled as bad rhetoric, or eloquence devoid of reason. So Cicero, in the *De inventione*, says that before the introduction of eloquence, "propter errorem atque inscientiam caeca ac temeraria dominatrix animi cupiditas ad se explendam viribus corporis abutebatur, perniciosissimis satellitibus" ("on account of error and ignorance, desire, the blind and reckless mistress of the mind, exploited to its satisfaction physical strength, the most pernicious of henchmen").[23] The lexical hierarchy here is clear and telling. At the bottom we find *cupiditas*, which led man, "propter errorem atque inscientiam," to satisfy its demands. This *cupiditas* is also *caeca* ("blind"), *temeraria* ("reckless"), and the *dominatrix* of the soul. In this state not only did passion (*cupiditas*) rule, but it was personified as a woman, while brute physical strength, the "satellite" of the *dominatrix*, was personified as male. Rhetoric gave to man *sapientia, ratio,* and *oratio* and so valorized his role while granting him control over *cupiditas*.

Here too Vergil reflects this rhetorical tradition, as Neptune's actions, in fact, result from the first persuasive act of the text: Juno's seduction of Aeolus (*Aen.* 1.65-75), where by offering a nymph for him to marry, she convinces him to do what she asks. Juno's rhetoric, every bit as effective as Neptune's, conforms to the opposing type of rhetoric, as it is not based on reason and philosophy, nor aimed at calming or teaching, nor motivated by a desire to invoke communion among men. Rather, she uses seduction to persuade Aeolus to let loose the horses of the winds—the same horses, perhaps, that are metaphorically brought to bay in the first simile. If

Neptune at this moment—and Aeneas shortly after—is modeled on the Isocratean orator, then Juno surely represents the pedlar of left-handed rhetoric of whom Plato so aptly disposes in the *Phaedrus*. And if Neptune is likened to the paradigmatic good man of whom both Isocrates and Cicero speak so highly, then Juno is, at the least, comparable to the figure these good men have supplanted in Cicero's mythological tale: *cupiditas*.

Initial conclusions would thus suggest that Vergil is proposing a world that corresponds to the one outlined in the Isocratean rhetorical tradition. Many have pointed out Vergil's own sympathies with rhetoric, calling him as much a rhetorician as a poet. Indeed, Gilbert Highet's *Speeches in the "Aeneid"* points out the degree to which speech and rhetoric are primary considerations of the epic.[24] And yet Vergil himself incorporates elements that question just such a conclusion: the satirical portrait of Drances, the only true orator in the text, which appears in book 11; the depiction on Aeneas' shield in book 8 of Cato, judging a trembling Catiline for treason, a passage assumed since the time of Servius to satirize Cicero.[25] If Vergil were really trying to insist that the world of the work was that of Isocrates and Cicero and that his ideals were comparable to theirs, there would be no purpose in including these antirhetorical elements. If, instead, he is trying to suggest the limits of such a system—setting it up carefully in order to attack it—then such inclusions can be justified.

The classical humanistic rhetorical tradition to which Vergil alludes in the first simile is, as we have seen, based on a certain set of relationships, a firm belief that humanity is set apart not by language alone but by the ability of a good man to persuade his audience, and a related conviction that this persuasion, based on reason, will bring about order from chaos, and community from isolation. As a result, however, certain equally human characteristics are ignored. Juno's initial actions, for example, are considered, by definition, to be worse than Neptune's; the speaker's crowd is depicted as *ignobile* and likened, even when calmed, to beasts. A hierarchy is established by the elevation and clustering of certain concepts, such as reason, language, and order, and, because of the moral cast granted the rhetorical institution, the inferior elements in each pair become associated with the bad. Above all, the method of good rhetoric (persuasion through speaking that instills order) is deemed appropriate, while its opposite (seduction, passion, even desire) is branded as immoral. Such a hierarchy is indeed powerful and effective, yet the humanist elevation of certain concepts, resulting in the rejection and denial of others, can create a system of priorities that is unbalanced and, ultimately, anything but humane.

By deliberately recalling not only the model of humanist oratory but the presence, strength, and force of *cupiditas*, Vergil establishes a context in which the rhetorical crisis (such as the one Cicero writes of in the *De inventione*) can be reconsidered and even, perhaps, rewritten in a way that is fairer to *cupiditas*; her tutelary goddess, Juno; and her various wards, including Dido, Camilla, and Turnus. The references in book 1 to a humanist worldview serve not to endorse that system but to introduce an etiology that needs rewriting. The *Aeneid* as a whole can thus be seen as at least a partial attempt at just such a rethinking of the assumptions of the rhetorical tradition.

2 JUNO'S DESIRE

Alta mente

In the last twenty years, scholarship of the *Aeneid* has shifted from viewing the text as a paean to Aeneas, Italy, and Augustus to showing increasingly the darker side of the text, the aspects that suggest the dangers of the Augustan system.[1] The two most eloquent of the "new" critics, M. C. J. Putnam and W. R. Johnson, have argued for reading the *Aeneid* as a political statement warning Augustus of potential dangers, as a text that not only celebrated the powers of rational man but also warned of the dangers involved in achieving a rule that necessitates the suppression of all subsidiary faculties, including passion.

While the political ambitions and beliefs of Cicero differed radically from those of Augustus, the method of their actions and the dynamics established between ruler and audience were certainly analogous.[2] For this reason—a thematic rather than historical one—I propose that a comparison of the humanist rhetorical model with Vergil's use of rhetoric could prove fruitful.

Putnam and Johnson take as one of their main targets the goddess Juno and suggest that a tremendous risk is run in suppressing her and her ilk. Yet both these critics insist ultimately that she is a negative figure;[3] both show her to be of a strength that must be reckoned with and not suppressed; both also indicate that she is a necessary evil.

Augustus presumably knew of the powers of Juno and all she stood for; otherwise he would not have suppressed rebellion with such vigor and would not have insisted on the superiority of reason. While I agree that the *Aeneid* is not a celebration of the status quo and that it does indeed introduce the problems of the darker forces, I would not agree that these forces need be viewed as negative. I would propose, rather, that Vergil is working within the current rhetorical system, that he is trying to suggest the limits of that system and, perhaps subconsciously, to escape from such a system, an effort in which he all but succeeds.

I will argue from the premise that Juno is meant not as the negative personification of the irrational but rather as the embodiment of all that is oppressed in a humanist world.[4] She is, in short, the *dominatrix animi,* and it is with her exile as much as with Aeneas' journey that the text concerns itself. That Vergil is interested in Juno can be seen from the start of the *Aeneid.* While the first eight lines introduce Aeneas, they do not employ a traditional or expected form. The *Iliad* and the *Odyssey,* the two other important epics upon which the *Aeneid* is modeled, both begin with an invocation to the muses. Vergil includes such an invocation, yet postpones it to line 8:

> Musa, mihi causas memora, quo numine laeso
> quidve dolens regina deum tot volvere casus
> insignem pietate virum, tot adire labores
> impulerit. tantaene animis caelestibus irae? (*Aen.* 1.8-11)

> Muse, remind me of the reasons: what divinity was harmed, why did she, the sorrowing queen of the gods, set in motion so many difficulties, so many trials for a man known for goodness. Is there such anger in heavenly minds?

Is this perhaps an indication that we are to see these lines as a second beginning of the text? If so, then we are faced with several problems. First, why not invoke the muses in the opening line? Second, why have two beginnings? Perhaps Vergil's text is really two epics. The first is indeed about Aeneas, arms, men, war, and all the trappings of a Ciceronian and rhetorically correct society, a Rome that both Cicero and Augustus would recognize and approve of . . . *in esse*. The second epic is Juno's, and it remains *in posse*. Since her will is not a valorized part of the world as it was rhetorically and socially structured, the language to express it does not exist. This may seem like a paraphrase of Putnam and Johnson, but I intend to push their ideas one step further. Not only does Juno represent the long-suppressed irrational, as character and symbol, she is the hero of the epic Vergil would have written and in part did write. Not only Juno is clearly frustrated; Vergil, too, is frustrated in his attempt to articulate the truth. It is worth remembering that Juno's epic has the true epic beginning.[5]

Moreover, it is Juno, not Aeneas, who is allowed the first speech of the text. She is thus the first to get our attention, and, more, her introduction and speech are written to elicit some sympathy for her, even if one is biased against her, as any Roman would most likely have been. Despite her recent victories at Troy, Juno remains hurt:

> manet alta mente repostum
> iudicium Paridis spretaeque iniuria formae
> et genus invisum et rapti Ganymedis honores (*Aen.* 1.26-28)

> in the depths of her mind remain implanted the Judgment of Paris and the injury to her spurned beauty; the hated race and honors given raped Ganymede.

Why mention this? There is no need to suggest that Juno has any motive for her anger beyond keeping Aeneas from Carthage. Yet these few lines add a significant dimension to her character. She is not just a goddess protecting her Carthaginian wards. She is a vulnerable figure who still carries with her, *alta mente,* unhealed wounds. Within a few lines she is thus transformed from Saturnia, daughter of Saturn, as she is first introduced, to a spurned and rejected lover, and the cause of her anger is allotted to this very human rejection with which we as readers can identify. That the pain she carries with her *alta mente* causes her anger is important since it is emblematic of her role in the text: such pain bears the same relation to her character as she does to the pantheon. Always frustrated, always suppressed ("et quisquam numen Iunonis adorat / praeterea aut supplex aris imponet honorem?" "and, henceforth, will anyone adore the glory of Juno or, kneeling at her altars, pay her honor?" as she says a few lines later), she can do nothing but erupt from the depths. She causes the pain in the system that her rejection causes her.

Juno's next action, in which she seduces Aeolus into creating a storm that causes Aeneas to shipwreck and lose some of his men, is usually used as proof of her destructive nature. She is rebellious, and she is indeed constantly causing pain to others. Yet how else can she react? What other role is she offered? Though sister and wife to Jove, she has never been granted due homage. This, more than keeping Aeneas from destroying Carthage, is her reason for opposing him so directly; she continues to war with him until he makes his peace with her. A character identified throughout Greco-Roman mythology with jealousy, spite, and rejection, Juno exists to give voice to the irrational forces within us. She is therefore not allowed to act in a rational way—such an act would be by definition out of character. In order to be heard she must erupt; her inferiority and irrationality are built into the structure of the pantheon. In other words, the explicit pantheon of the *Aeneid* reflects the hierarchy implicit in humanist rhetoric: reason is superior to passion; Jupiter is superior, at least at the start, to Juno, even though (or perhaps because) she is his sister and wife. The role she is allotted is the one she plays: she is the defining irrationality against which rationality and reason are highlighted and defined; without her Jupiter could not retain his superiority.[6]

Pulvis inscribitur

To view the *Aeneid* as, at least in part, an attack on the rhetorical paradigm is to present the work as a series of unfinished tales. Rather than viewing the epic through Aeneas' eyes, as it were, and following a continuous narrative from Troy to Latium, we will analyze the *Aeneid* from the perspective of the choices he rejects and follow where they lead. Such an approach is made entirely possible and justifiable by the fact that Vergil encourages us in this direction. Far from suggesting that the oppressed exist only to support the oppressor, he offers us time and again tantalizing and unfinished glimpses of the roads not taken. The prospects we see at these junctures—certainly not rhetorically apt—suggest other systems of thought.

Aeneas does not figure much in such an approach until the end. I see him as clearly established, from the start, as a developing Isocratean orator and an upholder of that system of values. Like Jupiter and Augustus, he sets the standard and provides the backdrop for the text. Juno, likewise, as the protagonist of the unfinished work, is only a model for a series of characters and scenes. Further, while the standard reading sees the text as building toward a tragic climax in Aeneas' murder of Turnus, I will view it more as a prewriting of a text that begins in the last line of the work. None of what occurs in the *Aeneid* matters as much as the very last line, and in that last line we are offered the first line of a new text that follows an entirely different set of assumptions.

My tracking of the Junonian traces in the *Aeneid* is not comprehensive. Rather, I wish to use a very limited reading as an indication of how embedded the rhetorical paradigm was and to what degree its mythology was under scrutiny. With this goal in mind, I have selected only those passages from the *Aeneid* that best serve to illustrate these points. I have chosen my examples from two major categories: those that speak to the necessity and possibility of a new paradigm and those that suggest what direction this new order will take.

Juno's temple

Soon after the speech that establishes Aeneas as orator, he finds himself at the temple of Juno built by Dido. Such a temple has rhetorical echoes that are worth calling up here. At the beginning of the second book of the *De inventione* Cicero says that the citizens of Croton wanted to paint a temple dedicated to Juno. They hired Zeuxis of Heraclea, considered the best, and he painted many panels. He also, however, wanted to include a painting of Helen, "ut excellentem muliebris formae pulchritudinem muta in se imago contineret" ("that would capture in its image the excelling beauty of her womanly form").[7] He asked the citizens to provide him with their most beautiful women to serve as models. He chose five, and from those five was able to assemble an image of the perfect woman, nature having given only some traits of perfection to each actual woman.

Cicero's Aristotelian source here is the *Poetics*. For even as Aristotle defines mimesis as depicting the probable if impossible, so Cicero asserts that in order to paint Helen, the epitome of beauty, the artist will gather a limited number of beautiful women and from them derive a painting of the most beautiful. She doesn't actually exist; she is impossible in the Aristotelian sense of the term. Yet as she is the logical extension of the five actual women, so the painting will be the logical or probable version of the impossible.

Vitruvius, whose treatise is modeled to a great extent on rhetorical works, refers, in his much-debated section on wall painting in book 7, section 5, of *De architectura,* to a like process:

> Namque pictura imago fit eius, *quod est seu potest esse,* uti
> homines, aedificia, naves, reliquarumque rerum, e quibus
> finitis certisque corporibus figurata similitudine sumuntur
> exempla. (italics mine)

> For the painting is the image of that which is or may be, for
> example, men, buildings, ships, and other things from
> whose definite and actual shapes like sketches are adopted.[8]

As with Cicero, the painting Vitruvius considers appropriate is
that which conforms to Aristotle's dicta of mimesis, that
which could or does exist. The paintings in bad taste are rather
"monstra potius quam ex rebus finitis imagines certae: pro
columnis enim struuntur calami striati . . . . Haec autem *nec
sunt nec fieri possunt nec fuerunt*" (italics mine) ("imaginary
creatures rather than certain representations of definite things:
so grooved reeds stand for columns . . . . Such things,
however, do not exist, nor cannot be, nor have existed").[9]
While Cicero asserts that there is only one way of painting,
Vitruvius acknowledges that there are more. Though Vitruvius would agree with Cicero that the mimetic method is best,
he acknowledges as well the existence of other approaches and,
consequently, of difference, a fact that Cicero, consciously or
not, suppresses.

Vergil seems to make a similar gloss on Cicero's text. The
temple to Juno in the *Aeneid* is covered with wall paintings of
scenes from the Trojan War. As Johnson and others have
pointed out, the reaction of Aeneas and his comrades recorded
by Vergil is not the reaction intended by the paintings: Juno's
temple presumably celebrates the Greek victory; Vergil, by
showing us the temple through Aeneas' eyes, tells us instead of
the Trojan loss.[10] Thus, art is shown to elicit varying responses
depending on the audience; both the paintings and the *Aeneid,*
the larger work of art in which the paintings appear, are open
to multiple readings.

Moreover, since we hear the Trojan version, not the Greek,
Juno's story once again goes untold. Yet her plight does not

remain entirely unnoticed, as one of the scenes described, that of Troilus, allows us to glimpse a figure much like Juno:

> infelix puer atque impar congressus Achilli,
> fertur equis curruque haeret resupinus inani,
> lora tenens tamen; huic cervixque comaeque trahuntur
> per terram, et versa pulvis inscribitur hasta. (*Aen.* 1.475-78)

unlucky boy, unequal match to Achilles, dragged by horses, he clings to the empty chariot, still holding the reins; his neck and hair are dragged through the dirt, and the dust is inscribed by his inverted sword.

This scene was meant to celebrate a victory of Achilles; it is described, however, as a disastrously unfair battle in which Troilus, much the weaker, is killed. Through the initial word of the description, *infelix,* Troilus is connected, albeit indirectly, with Juno; *infelix* is the word associated most often with Dido,[11] and the plights of Dido and Troilus are remarkably similar to that of Juno: all are pawns in unfair wars whose stories remain largely unfinished. The story of Troilus *inscribitur* with his inverted sword. Troilus' story is referred to as written passively: it is a tale that cannot be written out fully. Inscribed in the *Aeneid*, it is never fully told, for it tells of a pain too great to tell and a force too irrational to be put into words.

In a pantheon that gives Neptune and Jupiter clear power and duties and leaves Juno with nothing that is rightfully hers, stories of pain, fear, and rejection are stories that one expects to be omitted or told in an unsympathetic way. What is striking, however, is that Vergil does not suppress these stories as Cicero would presumably have done. Rather, Vergil makes us aware of their existence throughout the *Aeneid,* even if only briefly, and in what appears to be an offhand way: Juno's old hurt is frequently translated literally *entre parenthèses;* Troilus scribbles in the dust something we cannot read. In each instance, though the momentary glimpse of the untold story is followed by an image of repression, it never fully disappears.

While Juno's speech and outburst are followed by Neptune's subduing of the storm, and while the description of Troilus is followed by an image of Penthesilea, female warrior, what remains in our minds is the trace of a tale not yet told in full. Repeated use of this method leads the reader to expect such a pattern and increasingly to want the full tale to be spelled out.

The significance of the paintings in Juno's temple is, therefore, threefold. First, they show that art can mean more than it says, telling in miniature of the possibilities inherent in the text at hand. Second, they omit Juno's story. Third, they show a case in which pain is allowed to speak, however briefly, and in its passive, garbled speech to make a very eloquent plea for all the tales that remain untold.

Dido and the *Caecus ignis*

Dido is the most striking and tragic victim of the epic, and through her Vergil makes his most eloquent plea for change.[12] She appears while Aeneas is in Juno's temple studying the scenes from the Trojan War, and her arrival is given godlike flourish: she is presented as if she were Diana.[13]

Dido thus begins the text as a figure who is both removed and chaste, since she rules her city as a female king and oversees the building of its walls and turrets.[14] Through her love for Aeneas, she becomes a woman of nature, passion, and instinct. Once allowed to pursue her presumably innate desires, however, she cannot remain a part of the text. Vergil writes her out of it when he can no longer explain her; like the story of Troilus, her life story is only partially complete.[15]

On one level Dido is indeed a figure who interferes with Aeneas' journey to Rome. She is thus arguably a negative figure (or at the very least a temptation) in the epic. But this is not the Dido that Vergil offers us. Rather, he shows us a Dido who, though first introduced as invincible, becomes vulnerable. Before she falls in love she builds her city and prepares for war; she rules, in other words, in a way that supports the system. But once in love, Dido is transformed into a character who subverts the system. She does not become like Venus, a submissive female who, never at a loss for words, appeals to her father figure for support (as in *Aen.* 1.229-53). She becomes, instead, a sympathetic character guided by her emotions who is nonetheless not submissive. She is thus an anomaly in the rhetorical system and, more important, a threat to it.

Significantly, the progress of her transformation can be charted through her speeches. Eminently articulate at the start, speaking in a tone that aligns her with the male characters of Jupiter and Neptune, once in love she finds she cannot speak (*Aen.* 4.76) or finish her speeches.[16] This is not just evidence of dementia; it indicates as well that she cannot put into words what she is feeling. As we have already noted in Cicero,[17] such emotions do not build buildings or cities. And even when she does speak, it is a speech that begins with her eyes askance, a sign that she is unable to summon the rational powers necessary to combat Aeneas.

If Aeneas' reasons for leaving Dido are made clear, Vergil's reasons for staying are not. After Aeneas departs for Rome Dido plays no major part in the plot of the text; the bulk of book 4 could easily have been discarded. Rather than abandoning Dido when Aeneas does, however, Vergil stays with her, clearly sympathizing with her point of view as he shows the departure of the Trojans through her eyes and slowly marks her decline into magic and madness to her death on the funeral pyre. In both her own and the narrator's words, she becomes a tragic heroine of the Medea type.[18] Though Vergil ultimately writes her out of the text, he does so in the slowest and most painful way possible, showing not only a sympathy for her but a real ambivalence toward her character. In addition, she is not allowed to die an inglorious death: her suicide is officially sanctioned by Juno and thus, to a degree, by Vergil as well. His treatment of her is, in the end, perplexing. He needn't have dwelt on her; in killing her off, he needn't have done it so slowly. He seems both to want her out of the text—because she is at that point as much a threat to its rhetorical fabric as she is to Aeneas' fate—and to want her to remain because she represents something of value.

As many have pointed out, the images of fire used to describe Dido's fall in book 4 are instructive and help to explain this episode in the context of the work as a whole.[19] They become even more provocative, however, when compared to several passages from the rhetorical tradition. One phrase that links Dido directly with fire is *caecus ignis* ("blind flame"). Passion to Cicero was a *dominatrix* who was both *caeca* and *temeraria*. Vergil uses *caeca* elsewhere in his works in just that way: a passion so blind that it leads one to forget or overthrow reason. To use *caeca* as part of an image for passion is, at first blush, humanist. However, using it deliberately as an oxymoron—*caecus ignis* — suggests that the blindness is not without sight somewhere.

In this context it is also conceivable that Vergil used this motif not only to link Dido with the city-destroying fire of book 2 and the suicidal funeral pyre of book 4 but also to suggest that Dido's passion associates her with an alternative system of rhetoric that threatens the status quo. Such an alternative is alluded to in an interesting way in the rhetorical tradition preceding Vergil. Again Vitruvius is helpful: in the *De architectura* he includes an etiological tale that echoes Cicero's own founding myth:

> Homines vetere more ut ferae in silvis et speluncis et nemoribus nascebantur ciboque agresti vescendo vitam exigebant. Interea quodam in loco ab tempestatibus et ventis densae crebritatibus arbores agitatae et inter se terentes ramos ignem excitaverunt, et eius flamma vehementi perterriti, qui circa eum locum fuerunt, sunt fugati. Postea re quieta propius accedentes cum animadvertissent commoditatem esse magnam corporibus [ad] ignis teporem, ligna adicientes et id conservantes alios adducebant et nutu monstrantes ostendebant, quas haberent ex eo utilitates. In eo hominum congressu cum profundebantur aliter <atque aliter> e spiritu voces, cotidiana consuetudine vocabula, ut

obtigerant, constituerunt, deinde significando res saepius in usu ex eventu fari fortuito coeperunt et ita sermones inter se procreaverunt.

Men of old were born like wild animals in trees and caves and groves and survived on wild food. Meanwhile, in a certain place, the dense trees, blown by the storms and repeated winds, had excited a flame among the branches rubbing against each other, and those terrified by this wild flame who were anywhere around, fled. Subsequently, when things had quieted down, those approaching nearer became aware of the great comfort of the heat of the flame and added strewn branches, keeping it alive, added others, indicating with a nod how much comfort they got from it. In this group of men, where voices poured forth from the individual spirit, from daily habit they fixed on common nouns just as they had occurred, and by signifying things more often in use began, from this fortuitous event, to speak and so speech was created among them.[20]

What is of interest here is Vitruvius' curious attitude toward fire. He alludes to the Prometheus myth, which was frequently cited as the founding myth of civilization, but suggests that fire in its ambivalence could not civilize and that therefore its role was taken over by building:

Ergo cum propter ignis inventionem conventus initio apud homines et concilium et convictus esset natus, et in unum locum plures convenirent habentes ab natura praemium praeter reliqua animalia, ut non proni sed erecti ambularent mundique et astrorum magnificentiam aspicerent, item manibus et articulis quam vellent rem faciliter tractarent, coeperunt in eo coetu alii de fronde facere tecta, alii speluncas fodere sub montibus, nonnulli hirundinum nidos et aedificationes earum imitantes de luto et virgulis facere loca, quae subirent. Tunc observantes aliena tecta et adicientes suis cogitationibus res novas, efficiebant in dies meliora genera casarum.

Therefore, it was on account of the discovery of fire that originally caused community among men, both meetings and relationships were formed, and so as they kept coming together in greater numbers into one place, receiving from nature a gift surpassing the other animals, that not prone but erect they walked so that they could see the magnificence of the world and stars, so that they could drag with their hands and fingers easily the things they wanted, some began, in their coming together, to make shelters with leaves, others to hollow out caves on mountainsides, others, imitating nests of swallows and their structures, made shelters from mud and twigs. Then, looking at others' shelters, and adding new things of their own devising, they constructed, as the days progressed, better kinds of houses.[21]

Vitruvius glosses his version of the Prometheus myth to serve his own ends; building, not fire, was the true start of civilization. Yet his fleeting inclusion of the Prometheus myth helps point up its complete suppression in the Ciceronian passage. In the *De inventione* there is no direct mention of fire as a civilizing element. It does appear, however, in a seemingly offhand remark that precedes Cicero's etiological tale: "plurima bella restincta" ("many wars have been put out") by good rhetoric. Fire, he suggests, is neither civilizing, as the Prometheus myth would have it, nor ambivalent, as Vitruvius would suggest. It is instead purely negative and thus cannot be included in a founding myth. But why should the myth of Prometheus be so threatening? Here Vitruvius, in realizing a Ciceronian metaphor, points to an explanation. Fire had frequently been used as a metaphor for persuasion based on instinct and desire, as we will see in some detail later; this kind of communication—indeed, this whole approach to persuasion—may have posed a threat on some level to Cicero's humanist rhetoric, and so had to be suppressed altogether. Vitruvius, in his allusion to the Prometheus myth, makes clear Cicero's suppression.

While fire is ultimately destructive for Dido and links her on some level with the disastrous fires of Troy and Carthage, it is also, as Cicero's exclusion suggests, a metaphor for rhetoric and persuasion that function along other than rational lines, a communication that does not depend on speech alone or on the suppression of the passions. Vergil's references to Dido's inability to speak and its connection with fire may be an unconscious allusion to precisely this. But this rhetorical change is also indicative of a larger transformation: the altogether-too-brief period that she and Aeneas have together in Carthage is also the most sympathetic in the epic, as it speaks of a new order that emphasizes equality over control and balance over hierarchical suppression.

Finally, the image of fire is important because the blindness of the flames suggests, negatively, the bind in which she is caught and, positively, a possible way of understanding that bind in rhetorical terms. Calling a flame blind does not say only it is hidden; it also suggests that there is something to be seen that cannot be seen. Because the visual is understood consistently in both Vergil and the larger rhetorical tradition as the most rational of the senses, and because sight is often used as a metaphor for that sense, this particular oxymoron seems extremely telling. Not only is Dido's love one that can and cannot be seen, but it is a story that can and cannot be told.

Dido both bears the flame and becomes it. A living oxymoron, she is the invisible visible, the sight that cannot be seen. At this point, she does indeed become a danger to the text: she threatens to undermine the meaning of all language. For, as she becomes an example of what life would be like if passion were valorized, she also threatens the logic of language itself. As she becomes a *caecus ignis*, so she unites two opposites; she mediates between extremes and, in proving that such a mediation can occur, threatens to undo the hierarchical system that supports both the language and the social structure that Aeneas continues to uphold.

The story of Dido is developed at such length, I believe, as an extension of the same process that led Vergil to mention Juno's pain and Troilus' scribbling in the dust. Like them, Dido belongs to the part of the order that exists to be suppressed, the passion over which reason must rule triumphant. Aeneas' leaving of Dido at the bidding of Jupiter is further evidence for this contention, and for the strong existence of the hierarchy. Yet Vergil's sympathetic treatment of Dido, paired with his equally unsympathetic presentation of Aeneas at this point, suggests that Vergil finds such a system at fault. Instead of offering the rhetorically correct view, the story of Dido reconfirms Juno's sentiments as it makes the reader recognize both the pain of the oppressed and the possibilities that exist outside such a hierarchical order. By dwelling on the moment of leave-taking and its effect on the suppressed passion of both Dido and Aeneas, Vergil does something the rhetorical treatises never do: he informs us that this ritual act in which reason suppresses passion is neither constructive nor inevitable. While Aeneas may dwell on his need to go to Rome ("sed nunc Italiam magnam Gryneus Apollo / Italiam Lyciae iussere capessere sortes; / hic amor haec patria est . . . Italiam non sponte sequor" "But now Grynean Apollo orders me to take great Italy as do the Lycian prophecies; this is love, this the fatherland . . . I do not of my own will pursue Italy" [*Aen.* 4.345-47, 361]), Vergil allows us to see, once again, Aeneas' hesitation (*Aen.* 4.331-33) and, within that hesitation, the lie of such a necessity. Aeneas no more needs to go to Rome than reason "needed" to suppress *cupiditas*. Need is a handy excuse that Dido, and maybe even Aeneas, sees right through.

The story of Dido, then, reinforces a thematic established since the beginning of the text and make Vergil's subversive stance all the clearer. Even as he recognizes the existence of the cultural paradigm of rhetoric and power, Vergil also acknowledges that such a paradigm is neither all good nor essential. Through the character of Dido, he develops the sentiments first stated by Juno at the beginning of book 1 and makes it clear that if the systems, rhetorical and other, had been different, so would the sad story of Dido. Only because the system is structured as it is must Dido be written out of the plot.

Bis conatus

Throughout the *Aeneid* Vergil suggests ways in which the
assumptions of the humanist rhetorical system are limited.
Characters like Nisus and Euryalus and incidents such as the
death of Pallas speak directly to this problem, and, for the most
part, such criticism as Vergil makes follows the pattern
established in the stories of Troilus and Dido: a gentle nudging
of the audience, pointing to the pain of those suppressed,
accompanied by a suggestion that "Roman" ways are neither
unique nor best. But Vergil also had, I believe, a definite sense
of the direction in which he would have liked to see change
occur, even if he had no clearly formulated model in mind, and
this sense, hinted at in various places in the text, is spelled out
most directly in the final lines of the work.

In the last scene of the *Aeneid*, Aeneas kills Turnus out of
love for his friend and comrade Pallas and against the specific
precepts of his father. The action is dense and compact, and the
scene requires much reading and interpretation. It is arguably
the most perplexing scene of the work, as it ends the text
abruptly—some would say, too abruptly. The most interesting reading is that of M. C. J. Putnam, who notes that Aeneas'
going against his father's advice to "parcere subiectis et
debellare superbos" ("spare the humbled and bear down on the
proud") represents an acting out of the Daedalus and Icarus
story told in book 6.[22] Daedalus, escaping the labyrinth he has
constructed, warns his child in vain not to fly too close to the
sun; Icarus, disobeying, falls to the sea below. Aeneas, ignoring his father's advice, commits a similarly defiant act and kills
the humbled Turnus. In breaking out of his expected persona
of *pius Aeneas* and acting rashly and passionately, Putnam
argues, Aeneas becomes a tragic hero and the book ends.

I would suggest, instead, that the ending of the *Aeneid*, like
its beginning, is double. While Aeneas' story ends indeed with
the violent and tragic action of his killing Turnus, Vergil's
story ends with the death of Turnus and the voice of the

oppressed, not the oppressor. At the end, in other words, the text is focused not on Aeneas but on Turnus, and on his and Vergil's semiarticulate plea for a new system based on something other than the elevation of reason.

In discussing this final passage I am going to treat it as two separate events: Aeneas' decision to kill Turnus and Turnus' death. While the two are linked in a cause-effect relation, I will present them as separable attempts to end the text that parallel its two beginnings. Like the beginning, the ending incorporates two voices that speak to a single point and argue from two angles for a single, changed worldview.

One justification for such a separation of the final scene is that two different intertexts are involved. The first, which underlies Aeneas' decision, is, as Putnam noted, the story of Daedalus and Icarus as it is spelled out in book 6; the other, which fills out the death of Turnus, is the story of Camilla, told in books 7 and 11. Each of these events, and the subtexts they call up, will be treated separately; they will then be looked at together as the diptych that ends the text.

Daedalus and Vergil; Icarus and Aeneas

Aeneas' act of killing Turnus at the end of the *Aeneid* is indeed an echo of Icarus' actions as described in book 6. It also represents, however, a rewriting of the myth of Daedalus and Icarus, which is described in great detail at the start of book 6.

Many have noted the Janus-like function of book 6. Aeneas crosses many thresholds as he moves from the realm of the living to the realm of the dead, as he visits his father and confronts both his past and future. Book 6 also gives us many indications of the way in which what is to follow differs from what has already transpired, and much of that information comes from the ekphrasis at the start of the book. Here, too, we move from tales that lament the rhetorical paradigm to ones that point forward to a new model.

On the doors to the temple built by Daedalus for Apollo we find detailed Daedalus' exploits:

in foribus letum Androgeo; tum pendere poenas
Cecropidae iussi (miserum!) septena quotannis
corpora natorum; stat ductis sortibus urna.
contra elata mari respondet Cnosia tellus:
hic crudelis amor tauri suppostaque furto
Pasiphae mixtumque genus prolesque biformis
Minotaurus inest, Veneris monimenta nefandae,
hic labor ille domus et inextricabilis error;
magnum reginae sed enim miseratus amorem
Daedalus ipse dolos tecti ambagesque resoluit,
caeca regens filo vestigia. tu quoque magnam
partem opere in tanto, sineret dolor, Icare, haberes.
bis conatus erat casus effingere in auro,
bis patriae cecidere manus. (*Aen.* 6.20-33)

on the gates the death of Androgeos; then the Cecropidas
ordered to pay seven sons' bodies each year; the urn stands,
the lots having been chosen. Opposite, the Cnosian lands
rise from the sea: here Pasiphae's crude love for the bull, the
hidden mating, produced the Minotaur, mixed breed, two-
form offspring, monuments to perverted desire, here he
made the house and its inextricable path; Daedalus himself,
pitying the great love of the queen, solved the mazes and
wanderings of the palace leading the blind footsteps with a
string. You, also, Icarus, would have had a great part in such
a work, had sorrow allowed. Twice he tried to carve your
story in gold, twice the hands of the father stopped short.

On doors dedicated to Apollo, the god of reason and light, we
find depicted a strange story, or, more precisely, two strange
stories. First, there is the tale of the labyrinth, built and solved
by Daedalus, with its Minotaur at the center and Ariadne and
Theseus escaping from it by means of Daedalus' string. That
story is then glossed by a second one, told by Vergil though
not depicted by Daedalus, of his and Icarus' escape from the
labyrinth. Icarus does not follow the prescribed path, however, and when he flies too close to the sun (thereby testing both
Daedalus and Apollo), the wax on his wings melts and he falls,
lifeless, into the sea. If we view these tales as two versions of

the same story, they can be seen as proleptic of what will happen to Aeneas in the course of the sixth book as well as emblematizing rhetorical elements of the *Aeneid* as a whole.[23] For in this ekphrasis, as opposed to the one in book 1, the creator is both identified and depicted. More than the ekphrasis in book 1, then, this description focuses specifically on problems of creation—the relation of creator to audience and, by extension, of speaker to audience. Even though Daedalus creates in a visual medium, the process of ekphrasis causes such a visual work to be translated into a rhetorical medium, thus allowing the rhetorical issues followed so far to be foregrounded, and statements made about Daedalus' relation to his subject and work become applicable to Vergil and his work.

The first story explicitly involves Daedalus the inventor as he builds an inextricable labyrinth, a structure that is eminently rational, containing within it the Minotaur, a figure created from the blending of female and animal passion. Significantly, this monster is characterized by the phrase *crudelis amor*, a phrase used of Dido. In addition, Theseus escapes the clutches of this monster with Daedalus's help, much as Aeneas escaped from Dido. This suggests that the ekphrasis be seen at first as a reading of the Dido and Aeneas story. Like Theseus, Aeneas enters a virtually inextricable labyrinth in Carthage and almost gets caught; like Theseus as well, Aeneas escapes safely with the help of a father figure.

That this is only part of the story is made clear by the lines that follow. The second story shows Daedalus as unable to save—or portray—his son. This tale shifts the emphasis toward a father-son relationship— and toward Daedalus as artist, as he creates the wings in the story and the scenes on the doors—and so, I would suggest, serves as a gloss on the first tale, shifting the emphasis toward the characters of Aeneas and Anchises on the one hand and toward the *Aeneid* and Vergil on the other.

But whatever the doors actually "look" like, our version, glossed as it is by the narrator, shows Icarus ("tu quoque magnam / partem opere in tanto, sineret dolor, Icare, haberes" [*Aen.* 6.30-31]) and shows the pain caused to Daedalus ("bis conatus erat casus effingere in auro, / bis patriae cecidere manus" [*Aen.* 6.32-33]). Neither Icarus nor the pain is suppressed by Vergil. As with the other examples we have looked at so far, these doors are saying two things. While supporting the Apollonian powers of reason and poetry and the necessity for that reason to prevail on the literal level of the tale—what is actually depicted on the doors—they also show what Daedalus' art cannot show. Vergil's art, in contrast to that of Daedalus, includes Icarus and makes us aware of the pain Daedalus felt. The Minotaur, depictable in its negativity, is supplemented in our version by Icarus, who represents many of the same faculties, yet valorized. In Daedalus' tale Icarus is a threat to the system and so cannot be depicted. Vergil, however, includes Icarus in his version and, once again, shows a trace of a tale not fully told.

But in his inclusion of Icarus Vergil also rewrites the myth and changes its moral. Instead of emphasizing Icarus' error and wrongheadedness in willfully going against his father's precepts, Vergil suggests, in his direct address to Icarus, that such action has a place—that willfulness has value even if it causes pain, and that both the act and its consequence should be expressed.

As such, the tale speaks of what will come, for while the father figure of reason, in the forms of Jupiter and Mercury, "rescued" Aeneas from the man-eating passion of Dido and Carthage, it will not, the second story suggests, be able to do so in the future. Like Icarus, Aeneas will fly, against the specific precepts of his father, too close to the sun: as we have mentioned, and as others have pointed out, Aeneas' deliberate ignoring of Turnus' well-placed reminder of Anchises' advice (*Aen.* 6.853) to spare the defeated and bear down on the proud corresponds to Icarus' ignoring of Daedalus' command to fly the middle path.[24]

In many ways, it is true, Aeneas is modeled on Icarus: in his relation to a father figure—or a series of father figures—in his desire, expressed again and again throughout the book, to break out of the labyrinth of language. Though the incidents of hesitation and suppressed rebellion become less and less frequent as the book goes on, the potential for them remains. Aeneas is thus always a potential Icarus figure, though he is often essentially a Theseus figure; his Thesean qualities usually suppress and dominate over his Icarian ones—except at the end. Here Aeneas' Icarian side, the side that wills not to follow the precepts of his father and desires instead to pursue his own interests, to test the heat, not the light, of the sun—the passion not the reason—surfaces and is allowed to remain alive. For in this last moment, when Aeneas finally gives voice to all that has remained more or less successfully suppressed throughout the text, not only does Aeneas become Icarus, he resurrects Icarus. For unlike Icarus, he is allowed to leave the prescribed path and live to tell the tale.[25] Instead of having his wings melt and falling to the sea below—in place of discovering that the sun of passion is necessarily harmful—Aeneas escapes alive.

Yet he does not escape unscathed; faced with the choice between his father's precepts and his love for a dead friend he is really offered—both historically and textually—a choice between Roman and Greek. Through the act of killing Turnus in cold blood, Aeneas becomes a Greek rather than the Roman hero he was meant to be, as his action here is modeled on that of Achilles, who kills Hektor to avenge Patroklos.[26] In choosing to disobey the words of his father and fatherland and to avenge the death of a friend, he reverts to the *Iliad*. He has, it is suggested, no other options, and in his decisively anti-Roman move of killing the humbled Turnus he becomes Greek.

If the text had ended here this would be a regression. But Vergil does not end it at this point. Instead, he supplements Aeneas' actions with the final event of the text, the death of Turnus. In addition to considering Aeneas' action at the end of the work, we must consider Vergil's motivation for his final depiction of Turnus and his final words of the text.[27]

The last line of the epic reads: "vitaque cum gemitu fugit indignata sub umbras" ("and, with a groan, his life, unavenged, fled to the shades below" [*Aen.* 12.952]).[28] To understand this line we have to set it in its context—which includes not only the immediate circumstances surrounding Turnus' death but also an earlier series of events: the same line is used of Camilla's death in book 11.[29] Given the self-consciousness with which Vergil repeats important phrases, this repetition suggests that a study of Camilla would be instructive.

Camilla is introduced at the end of book 7, which is notable for being the first book of the second, "greater" half of the text and for its focus on women:[30] it begins with the burial of Aeneas' nurse, Caieta ("Tu quoque litoribus nostris Aeneia nutrix,/ aeternam moriens famam, Caieta, dedisti" "You, also, Aeneas' nurse Caieta, in dying gave to our shores eternal glory" [*Aen.* 7:1–2]); proceeds to evoke a second muse, Erato, introducing the Latin women Lavinia and Amata[31] and the fury Allecto; and ends with the description of Camilla. The progression is significant, for Aeneas' nurse is replaced by his enemy: his mother figure by a woman who is every bit his equal and rival.[32] Whatever women stood for in the first half of the text thus implicitly undergoes a metamorphosis, a rebirth that, given the position of this book, implies that the new woman born out of the burial of the old represents the spirit of this second and final part.

So who is this new woman? How is Camilla first described? Her introduction is worth quoting at length:

Hos super advenit Volsca de gente Camilla
agmen agens equitum et florentis aere catervas,
bellatrix, non illa colo calathisve Minervae
femineas adsueta manus, sed proelia virgo
dura pati cursuque pedum praevertere ventos.
illa vel intactae segetis per summa volaret
gramina nec teneras cursu laesisset aristas,
vel mare per medium fluctu suspensa tumenti
ferret iter celeris nec tingeret aequore plantas.

illam omnis tectis agrisque effusa iuventus
turbaque miratur matrum et prospectat euntem,
attonitis inhians animis ut regius ostro
velet honos levis umeros, ut fibula crinem
auro internectat, Lyciam ut gerat ipsa pharetram
et pastoralem praefixa cuspide myrtum. (*Aen.* 7.803-17)

Beside these Camilla of the Volscian nation arrives, leading a squadron of horsemen and troops bright with brass. A female warrior, her feminine hands were not accustomed to the basket or distaff of Minerva; a virgin toughened instead to suffer war and to outstrip the winds in running. She flies across the tops of untouched grain—and does not mar the tender ears—or poised on the breaking wave she goes over the sea, her swift soles not touching the water. The youths all come out to see her passing, from the houses and the fields; the crowd of matrons admire and watch her, gasping in astonishment at how the regal purple covers her smooth shoulder, how the fibula interweaves her hair with gold, how she herself carries the Lycian quiver, the pastoral myrtle on her pointed spear.

Camilla is described in such a way as to suggest she is to be compared not just with men but also with the gods: outstripping the winds, she flies over field and sea.[33] In particular, these words link her with the god Mercury; when Mercury is described in book 4 it is said that "pedibus talaria nectit / aurea, quae sublimem alis sive aequora supra / seu terram rapido pariter cum flamine portant" ("he binds golden sandals on his feet which, winged, carry him aloft over land and sea, swift as the rapid gales [*Aen.* 4.239-41]). Mercury and Camilla, both described with touches of gold, fly swift as the wind equally well over land and sea.

Moreover, there is an etymological connection between Mercury and Camilla. Servius, in his commentary on the *Aeneid*, explains that a servant (*minister*) is called either *camillus* or *camilla*, "unde et Mercurius etrusca lingua Camillus dicitur, quasi minister deorum" ("hence Mercury is called Camillus in the Etruscan, as if a servant of the gods").[34] Macrobius has his character Servius repeat this etymology in the *Saturnalia* (3.8.7). But he adds the words "flaminicarum et flaminum prae ministros" ("as servants of priests and priestesses").[35] This addition is significant in establishing a link between Mercury and Camilla, for *flamen* has a second meaning, "blast of wind," and, as we saw above, Vergil uses this word to describe Mercury's speed: "rapido pariter cum flamine" (*Aen.* 4.241: "swift as the rapid gales").

But why Mercury? In standard mythology Mercury is the god who leads men to the underworld, god of the crossroads, god of commerce, and god of rhetoric.[36] He is thus a complex figure; perhaps the single unifying thread is his function as a go-between, a mediator who is able to make transitions and help others do the same, whether it be from one world to the next or one mode of existence to another. In the *Aeneid*, however, his role is limited to that of mediator between Jupiter and Aeneas: most particularly, he is the one sent by Jupiter to persuade Aeneas to leave Dido (*Aen.* 4.265ff.). He is thus not only an orator par excellence but the orator of the Roman cause. He appeals to Aeneas' rational capacity and convinces him to put aside his love for Dido for the sake of the future of Rome (*Aen.* 4.272-76). He therefore represents and upholds the divine plan and the system that insists on the priority of both Jupiter and Aeneas.

Camilla serves a comparable function in the cause of the unwritten text. She, too, is a mediator between earth, water, and sky; hair and gold; pastoral and war—significantly, myrtle entwines her spear. She thus represents the spirit of the Latins in her blending of pastoral peace and war, but she also modulates between the two in a way that is uniquely hers. She is a woman who is faster than men, yet still admired by other, particularly maternal, women. She thus mediates between men and women, pastoral and civic, peace and war, in a way that Mercury never could. For whereas Mercury's mediation in Vergil is always a process of rational direction, Camilla would seem, judging from the above description, to tread a middle ground, truly to mediate between two extremes.

In Ciceronian terms, Mercury helps Aeneas replace the *dominatrix cupiditas* of Dido with the rational and rhetorically possible goals of creating a civilized Rome, the goals that he was nominated to fulfill. Camilla, on the other hand, gains attention by blending opposites in her person, in her motion, and in her attributes. As such, she implies the presence of a force that wins favor in an unrhetorical way. She is, in sum, a positive female figure whose presence implies that success can be attained through something other than suppression of the extreme opposite.

The story of Camilla's childhood, her etiological tale, which is told before she is killed in book 11, bears out this initial impression. Her father, caught in a battle, bound her to a lance, dedicated her to Diana, and sent her across the flooded stream that stood between them and safety. Growing up in pastoral surroundings she chose to remain a virgin in spite of many mothers' wanting her as daughter-in-law. She represents, therefore, a perfect blend of opposites: her powers are not aimed at expelling the noncivilized in favor of the rational and civilized; rather, she stands for a reversion to the pastoral. While in Cicero's mythology this was the time of chaos and the reign of animal passion, preceding as it did the creation of institutions such as rhetoric, for Camilla this is the preferable time, an epoch whose positive side she embodies and, most important, whose qualities she is able to retain and blend with civilization. She is thus, above all, a positive *dominatrix*, a figure who stands for a new and different relation between opposing forces.

In the discussion of Juno's temple I drew an analogy between Vitruvius and Vergil, suggesting that Vitruvius marks the limits of his discourse by alluding negatively to what lies beyond the approved system, while Vergil marks those limits by looking to the areas outside in a neutral or even wistful way. Camilla, I would suggest, inhabits and personifies one of those areas without. Vergil, like the mothers and youths, admires her as she passes by.

As sympathetic as Vergil is to Camilla and what she stands for, he is also threatened by her, and as such shows his Roman colors most clearly. For as positive a figure as she cuts in her introduction, she, like all the Junonian characters in the *Aeneid*, is not allowed to realize her potential. Rather, she is written out of the text, killed on the battlefield while chasing down Chloreus for his armor. The reason for her death, the death of one who is in all other ways, Vergil suggests, invincible, is ascribed to the fact that "femineo praedae et spoliorum ardebat amore" ("she was burning with the feminine love of booty and spoils" [*Aen.* 11.782]). Instead of allowing Camilla to remain the character she was in her introduction, Vergil turns her into a stereotype and has her fall victim to a womanly passion. Even though Vergil introduces her as the new woman, replacing and adjusting the old by the new, and suggests that she is the spirit of a new system, the new Mercury of a new order, he cannot write her fully into the text. She holds great promise that he cannot allow her to fulfill; rather than the messiah of a new order she resembles at her initial description, she becomes proof of the truth of an existing order. She dies because of her *cupiditas*, the text insisting that beneath it all she is a woman like the others and that for her *cupiditas* she deserves to be eradicated.

Yet she is still a character in the text. Her tale, like that of Troilus, is partially written. And more, the final line of the text—its absolute last word—recalls the image and tale of Camilla. Vergil is thus asking us to see Turnus as a Camilla and so to remember her.

Turnus, too, represents a new order. Like Camilla, he is presented as a blend of pastoral and civic; he fights out of his love for Lavinia, a love that far surpasses any that Aeneas shows for her. Moreover, even though we are clearly biased against Turnus from the start, he, like Camilla, is allowed such a sympathetic portrayal that we can not write him off. In addition, he is meant to fight for and represent Juno's forces and so is set in direct opposition to Aeneas: Turnus is called to arms by women, Aeneas by men, Turnus by forces from the underworld, Aeneas by forces from Olympia.[37]

With his dying groan Turnus utters a plea for vengeance and a call for Juno to return. At this stage in the work she has removed herself from the action, and Aeneas and Turnus are left up to their own devices. This, I feel, is extremely significant, for Aeneas kills Turnus by himself, unmotivated by any god; Juno is not responsible for this act. By absolving Juno from any association with this final scene, Vergil is able to show that Juno is more a victim than a perpetrator. She is not the author of these actions; she is not the embodiment of cruel irrationality; she is not, in short, *dominatrix animi*. Rather, it is the structure that is at fault, the system that needs a scapegoat who is simultaneously responsible and powerless. Throughout the text the assumption has been made that Juno was responsible for all (negative) irrational actions, that Juno could do nothing right, and that all inspired by her were equally flawed. By the same token, she was denied all power and all chance to prove otherwise. Yet by removing her from the text Vergil finally tells us that it is not she who is responsible; it is Aeneas, it is everyman.

To reinforce this statement we are offered Turnus' unavenged soul and groan. We as reader are meant to avenge his unplayed life, to give voice to the unspoken passions that run like a river beneath the surface of the text. Juno is as much a hero as Aeneas—perhaps more so—though neither succeeds fully. She is both author and passive victim; she is the agent of what is inscribed. The text Vergil wanted to write had to remain the passive, unplayed text. Any time it rose to the surface, came close to being recognizable, it was suppressed, and the character or author of that plot written out. Only at the end, when left to his own devices, is Aeneas finally able to disrupt the rhetorical paradigm, and only then is there hope for a restructuring of the ways of language and of art. Significantly, it is Vergil who at this point falls silent. Like Aeneas, he makes his final gesture; it is the one that is not aborted or rewritten in the language of the system. Once made, the text must end; he cannot write out his masterpiece.

But the last line has further ramifications. Through his parallel depictions of Camilla and Turnus, Vergil suggests that non-Roman need not be Greek. While Aeneas may have had only two choices, Roman or Greek, Turnus, like Camilla, seems to represent a new system of values and priorities that, while definitely not Roman, are also not Greek. While the message Aeneas' action points to is the regressive and tragic one of the *Iliad*, the message of the *Aeneid*—Vergil's last word—points forward to a new, non-Ciceronian, non-Roman system that emphasizes balance and mediation. A rhetoric remains, I would suggest, the ruling paradigm, but Mercury's rhetoric has been replaced by Camilla's.

The ending of the *Aeneid* thus mirrors its beginning. Even as the text began, I would contend, twice—first with the introduction of Aeneas and his Ciceronian priorities, then with an introduction to Juno through her opening speech—so it ends twice, first with Aeneas' rewriting of the Icarus myth by ignoring the paternal advice, killing Turnus for the memory of Pallas, and living beyond the act, then with the death of Turnus itself. At both the beginning and the end the two stories work as do the tales on Daedalus' doors: the first is humanistic and morally apt, the second a less-approved version that serves as corrective gloss through which Vergil makes clear his own preferences. In the beginning Aeneas' mission is supplemented by Juno's needs; in the end Aeneas's choice is supplemented by the deaths of Camilla and Turnus.

Vergil ends the epic as he began it, *bis conatus*, as he gives the oppressed the first and last utterances of the text. Not only do these glosses suggest a sympathy on his part for a non-Roman, non-Ciceronian order, but the very fact that he glossed both beginning and end points to a form of oration that is other than humanist. In doubling both and in making the text come full circle, he subverts the true sense of beginning and ending. Instead of an architectonic structure with a clear start and finish, Vergil's epic has a circular structure that is more organic. It suggests an undermining of precisely the kind of distinction classical rhetoric depends upon, and in its blurring of essential formal elements, it suggests the qualities that characters such as Camilla represent. A sense of transformation and mediation, not of distinction and oppression, prevails at the end of the text.

The message of the *Aeneid*, then, is that we, like Icarus, need an art that does more than the Roman *artes* given us by Anchises: we need to do more than spare the suppliant and bear down on the proud. We need, in short, to come up with an art that does not hierarchize in such a way as to divide the world into the suppliants and the proud, or into passion and reason, for as liberating as Anchises' words seem in the general context of the text, they nonetheless do little to restructure the system of thought. Instead, Anchises' words advocate a reinforcement of the extant hierarchy. By insisting on a duality posited between proud and humble—a duality that translates into that of reason and passion, Jupiter and Juno—Anchises' words do not resolve a thing. All people in power will judge those most like them to be the humble, those unlike, the proud. Juno, for instance, gains nothing from this dictum: her actions, provoked out of anger and frustration, will appear to those in power as the actions of the proud; those on the bottom can be judged as nothing but proud as they fight for rightful dignity and acknowledgment by those in power, while those on top can only be judged humble, as they have nothing more to aspire toward, and can defer at every instance. What the *Aeneid* pleads eloquently for is a system in which pride need not be humbled. Aeneas' actions are a step in that direction; as a resurrected Icarus, Aeneas paves the way for the rewriting of myths such as those of the supreme powers of reason and the consequent danger of passion. By using every form of persuasion to attack the Roman *artes*, Vergil makes clear the limits and drawbacks of such an order.

Vergil also, as I have suggested, points in the direction in which such a new system—a new Roman rhetoric or art— would develop. Such an order, as I have tried to show, would allot Juno a rightful and valorized place in the new pantheon, would allow characters such as Dido, Camilla, and Turnus to be played out, and would allow what was written in the dust to be spelled out in marble and gold, as it would somehow give voice to what had been kept silent for so long. He comes closest to actually doing this himself in the characters and passages that prove most problematical and in his use of ambivalent allusions, such as the various ekphrases and meta- phors like *caecus ignis*. He emphasizes repeatedly the need for mediation—in character, in style, in plot, and in the world— and for an intellectual framework and language that would allow for such mediation to find voice. His work, therefore, shows most strongly the inadequacies of the old yet, at the same time, suggests, however tentatively and in however incomplete a fashion, one possible method for achieving a true new.

It is interesting to note, in closing, that it is in Vergil's fourth Eclogue that he came closest to realizing this new goal. Here, in a poem that he claims is written in a new style, he speaks of a new order in which mediation plays a far greater role than does hierarchy. The poem ends with the birth of a child, like the end of the *Aeneid*, which ends with a groan, a birthpang of the new system.[38] I bring up this poem not only because it does play out, in miniature, many of the unwritten themes of the *Aeneid* but also because it is the reason that throughout the Middle Ages Vergil was revered as prophet, for this fourth Eclogue was read as a prediction of the coming of Christ.[39] If only in rhetorical terms, his *Aeneid*, like his fourth Eclogue, did exactly that.

PART TWO
The Hermeneutics of Charity

3 AUGUSTINE AND THE REINCORPORATION OF DESIRE

Augustine's Vergil

When Augustine was in school in Carthage he won a prize, he tells us in the *Confessions*, for reciting a prose paraphrase of Juno's opening speech from the first book of the *Aeneid:*

> ut dicerem verba Iunonis irascentis et dolentis, quod non possit Italia Teucrorum avertere regem. . . . ille dicebat laudabilius, in quo pro dignitate adumbratae personae irae ac doloris similior affectus eminebat, verbis sententias congruenter vestientibus. ut quid mihi illud, o vera vita, deus meus? quid mihi recitanti adclamabatur prae multis coaetaneis et conlectoribus meis? (1.17)

> I had to recite the speech of Juno, who was pained and angry because she could not prevent Aeneas from sailing to Italy. . . . The contest was to be won by the boy who found the best words to suit the meaning and best expressed feelings of sorrow and anger appropriate to the majesty of the character he impersonated. Why did all this matter to me, my God, my true Life? Why did my recitation win more praise than those of the many other boys in my class?[1]

Augustine's acknowledged identification with, and empathy

for, Juno's first words, told here in the first book of the *Confessions*, suggests an interesting connection between Augustine and Vergil. By reciting Juno's speech Augustine briefly becomes Juno and voices the battle cry that instigates the action of the *Aeneid*; by playing Juno Augustine is also ritually calling out to be heard, just as Juno asks to be heard; one can even infer that—at least for the time of the recitation, if not for all of the first eight books of the *Confessions*— Augustine becomes Juno as a way of asking not to be suppressed, ignored, and forgotten. That the speech is not quoted but is only referred to makes its function as voice of the suppressed even clearer. This is an angry cry for attention that the unconverted Augustine feels he must make but that the converted Augustine, who writes the book, only alludes to. The voice of the suppressed, it is perhaps internalized as the voice of his conscience and of the fighting part of his soul, which will ultimately lead to his conversion. The sociopolitical drama Vergil plays out through the plot of the *Aeneid* is here presented as a psychological struggle; the various voices and roles Augustine assumes throughout the *Confessions* suggest an internal battle—a sort of psychomachia.

The *Confessions* is not only the story of one life; it is the story of the conversion of an entire culture from one that set as its model the Isocratean orator to one that recognized the necessity of desire to rhetoric and tried to valorize its role. Augustine's transformation of the *Aeneid* and the rewriting of certain Vergilian myths that surface in the *Confessions* help us understand in a literary, ideological, and rhetorical context the great shift in the rhetorical contract that had occurred between the writing of the two works.[2]

That Augustine, the protagonist of the *Confessions*, assumes even momentarily Juno's voice indicates that his text may be a transformation and rewriting of the *Aeneid*. By altering scenes taken from the *Aeneid* he acknowledges a connection with that work and, I would suggest, offers an answer to the cries and pleas found there.

The most telling example comes when Augustine leaves Carthage. Other critics [3] have noted that the scene is parallel to that of Aeneas' leaving Carthage and Dido. Augustine, like Aeneas, leaves Carthage for Rome; Augustine's mother, Monica, like Dido, is shown to be weeping as he leaves: "She wept bitterly to see me go and followed me to the water's edge, clinging to me with all her strength in the hope that I would either come home or take her with me" (5.8). But there are differences here, and a cluster of intertextual allusions in both the story from the *Aeneid* and the version presented in the *Confessions* help explain how we are to understand this parting scene. In the *Aeneid*, Dido's abandonment and experimentation with black magic are strongly reminiscent of the story of Medea. [4] In Ovid's version of the Medea myth (*Metamorphoses* 7.2–73.), drawn from that of Apollonius of Rhodes and presumably close to the one Vergil would have known, Medea falls in love with Jason, against her better judgment, and is abandoned by him. She develops her talents in magic to try to restore him to her. The parallels with the Dido story are obvious, but there is one major difference: the ending. Whereas Dido kills herself upon losing Aeneas, Medea's response is to make herself wings and fly off to the distant land of Aegeus where she begins life anew, at least for a while. Medea thus not only remains alive but is in a sense reborn. Dido is not so lucky.

As we pointed out in the last chapter, however, Dido's experience is not unique in the *Aeneid*. The path her life takes, her obsession with Aeneas, for which Vergil offers both a sympathetic reading together with an abrupt and absolute ending as he writes her out of the plot, is paralleled by the stories of Camilla, Aeneas, Turnus, and, most important for the present purposes, Icarus. Of that list, only Aeneas is allowed to live; instead of killing Aeneas, Vergil kills the plot and ends the story. By cutting off the epic at this point Vergil offers without comment a revised version of the other similar stories, essentially rewriting the Icarus myth to allow Icarus to survive his flight. As a parting shot Vergil offers the surviving Aeneas, the new Icarus.

It would seem that Augustine's response to these characters is in keeping with what Vergil suggested at the end of the *Aeneid*, for he identifies not only with Juno but also with Medea: "volantem autem Medeam etsi cantabam" ("I used to recite verses about Medea's flight through the air") (3.6). His choice of Medea is significant because of her connection with Dido and because she survives her trials. The reference to Medea comes shortly before Augustine leaves Carthage, and we are clearly meant to see it in the context of Dido and Aeneas, as Augustine refers at length to that story earlier in the text and thus makes it part of the narrative context. Yet by referring to Medea rather than Dido at this point, Augustine is offering a lens through which we can understand his version of the Dido-Aeneas story. While it starts as a direct calque from *Aeneid* 4—like Aeneas, Augustine leaves his beloved weeping on the shore to pursue another, higher glory—there is a significant difference from the Dido-Aeneas story that points to an important intertext. Monica is not Augustine's lover. As complex as the relationship is, she is still his mother, his authority figure and guide. Their relationship is thus as close to that of Daedalus and Icarus as it is to that of Dido and Aeneas: as Augustine leaves against his mother's wishes, so Aeneas leaves the unwilling Dido and, most important, like Icarus flies away from the prescribed path. Augustine is thus not just the Aeneas of book 4, he is also the Aeneas of book 12—a rewritten Icarus figure who survives, in spite of disobeying parental orders. Further, by offering the Medea story as an intertext, Augustine suggests a new way of understanding this departure. He is indeed the new Icarus, the Icarus that Aeneas becomes in book 12, but that Icarus is none other than Medea.[5] By transforming the gender from male to female, from Icarus to Medea, he becomes both the surviving Icarus and the surviving Dido, the character that need not be written out of the plot. He does not die, either in the flames of the sun or in those of the funeral pyre.

Neither, however, does his mother die in flames. She too, like a second Medea, leaves Carthage to follow Augustine, first to Rome, then to Milan. Monica, too, becomes more a Medea than a Dido; she rewrites Dido's plot so that it follows more closely the plot of Medea. The Medea story that forms the background to the Dido plot in the *Aeneid* is foregrounded here by Augustine. Even as Aeneas becomes both the new Icarus and the new Medea, so Monica plays out the fulfilled Dido, not the foreshortened, frustrated version found in the *Aeneid*.

From these brief examples, then, one can see that the *Confessions* provides at least to a limited extent an answer to the *Aeneid*. What the *Aeneid* inscribes and implots to the fullest of its ability, the *Confessions* writes out; what the *Aeneid* asks for the *Confessions* supplies. Instead of reading the *Confessions* as primarily autobiographical, we should see it as the record of a cultural change: the transformation chronicled for us in this text is emblematic of a much larger ideological one.[6] Thus it is significant that Augustine uses an orator as his protagonist, or, rather, that he considers his autobiography, that of a pagan orator turned Christian preacher, to be a suitable vehicle for telling the transformation of a culture. The model of power and suppression that the *Aeneid* both wants to support and tries to subvert is subverted by Augustine's conversion. Our comparison of rhetorical systems is facilitated by the fact that in the *Confessions*, more than in the *Aeneid*, rhetoric is clearly central to the plot: Augustine began life as an orator and ended it as a preacher. He presents the orator as the model on which he fashioned himself and developed as a child.[7] He is talking, therefore, not just about his own development but also about that of the culture of which he is part, a culture that changed its perception of itself and its ideals, and did so in ways that can be understood in terms of a rhetorical model.

As an orator, Augustine perceived the world and its fundamental relationships in terms of rhetoric, and we will return to
his particular formulations of these transformations at the end
of this chapter. But the reorganization of elements necessary to
the rhetorical contract occurred long before Augustine; in
many ways he was little more than a cataloger or theoretician
of an existing state, much as Cicero had been for his worldview. Also like Cicero, Augustine articulates in his rhetorically
based texts a set of standing assumptions that had been guiding
the choices of many for centuries before him. What Augustine
translates into highly rhetorical and learned terms is an intel-
lectualization of a shift in the ideological paradigm of his
culture.

As is often the case, the place to learn of such a fundamental
shift in perception is not the later, overdetermined interpretations but earlier attempts to articulate what is new. Such are
the paintings of the Roman catacombs.

Rhetoric of Participation: The Roman
Catacomb Paintings and the
Protevangelium of James

Analysis of catacomb paintings is made extremely problematical by virtue of their historical marginality—we know little
of who painted them and what for.[8] Jerome does, however,
offer an interesting insight into how he viewed them:

Dum essem Romae puer, et liberalibus studiis erudirer,
solebam . . . diebus Dominicis sepulcra apostolorum et
martyrum circuire; crebroque cryptas ingredi, quae in ter-
rarum profunda defossae, ex utraque parte ingredientium
per parietes habent corpora sepultorum et ita obscura sunt
omnia, ut propemodum illud propheticum compleatur:
Descendant ad infernum viventes; et raro desuper lumen
admissum, horrorem temperet tenebrarum, ut non tam
fenestram, quam foramen demissi luminis putes: rursumque

pedetentim acceditur, et caeca nocte circumdatis illud Virgilianum proponitur: Horror ubique animos, simul ipsa silentia terrent.

When I was a boy at Rome, and was being educated in liberal studies, I was accustomed . . . to visit on Sundays the sepulchres of the apostles and martyrs. And often did I enter the crypts, deep dug in the earth, with their walls on either side lined with the bodies of the dead, where everything is so dark that it almost seems as if the psalmist's words were fulfilled: *Let them go down alive into hell* (Ps. 55.15). Here and there the light, not entering through windows, but filtering down from above through shafts, relieves the horror of the darkness. But again, as one cautiously moves forward, the black night closes round, and there comes to mind the line of Vergil:

Surrounding horrors all my soul affright
And more, the dreadful silence of the night. [*Aen.* 2. 755].[9]

Clearly the catacombs caught Jerome's imagination, and in a very telling way for our purposes: to him they were the repository of the darker forces of the *Aeneid*. Quoting from book 2, at the moment when Aeneas returns to find Creusa, Jerome likens the catacombs to the outer darkness of the fall of Troy and, implicitly, to the inner darkness of the pain and loss of a loved one.

The catacombs Jerome is referring to date from the second century; the majority of the paintings were executed in the third and fourth centuries. The style of the paintings, though frequently rough and crude, shows similarities with the contemporary Roman painting;[10] traces of each pagan style can be found in the catacombs. Yet what the catacomb painter seems to have been interested in was promoting a certain truth, not developing a certain style or painting technique, and this truth and its method of presentation remain fairly consistent throughout the centuries.

The best proof of this is the striking fact that the majority of paintings depict Old Testament rather than New Testament scenes. Assuming that the catacombs were not only for Jewish burial, one has to explain this fairly unusual phenomenon. Fear of persecution is really not a feasible explanation; if that were the case, there would be no New Testament scenes at all, and there are some in every catacomb. So why the emphasis on Old Testament stories?

The scenes from the Old Testament that appear most frequently are those of Jonah, Noah, Daniel, and Susanna, all types of the Resurrection, a suitable subject for a Christian burial spot.[11] Yet just to point out the typological relationship between an Old Testament scene and a New Testament implied reading really begs the question. What a typological situation does is assert a particular relationship between the work and its audience. Shown a picture of Jonah, for instance, one might respond: "Type of resurrected Christ." The work has said something "out loud," as it were, and the viewer has responded by assigning it a second name or title. The suggestion in all such situations is that what is seen—or said—is not the full truth or meaning. Such truth is established only after the audience has participated enough to supply something. This participation—little more than an involuntary reaction—completes the communication while allowing the participant to experience the truth. Conversely, the full truth of the painting remains unstated and unseen.

Other paintings in the catacombs also suggest the necessity for this type of reading—what Grabar has labeled an image-sign.[12] A fair number of the scenes show a combination of figures that suggests a symbolic relation.[13] In each case the pairing is clear, though it is never explicit; you have to know something of Christianity to understand fully the meaning of the paintings. For instance, figure 2, a scene from the *Coemeterium Maius* in which Adam and Eve are separated not only by the tree of the knowledge of good and evil but also by the healed paralytic holding up his bed, suggests that the action of the Fall has been redeemed by a miracle, that Christ has saved us from the Fall. Similarly, a scene from the catacomb of

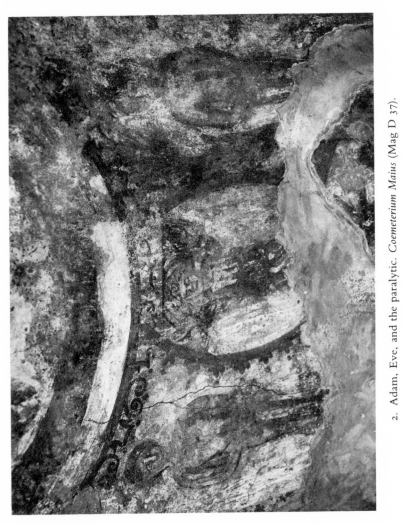

2. Adam, Eve, and the paralytic. *Coemeterium Maius* (Mag D 37).

Priscilla shows a Madonna and child together with an angelic figure, read either as the angel Gabriel or the prophet from Isaiah; in either case there is a conflation of scenes: a prophecy depicted with its fulfillment. In these instances the audience must supply the organizing matrix. In and of themselves these paintings make no narrative sense: if the two stories involved in each case are not known, or if the constant that makes such a pairing is not understandable, then these scenes become meaningless.

That the catacomb paintings involve a fairly rigorous inter-pretative mechanism is indicated, then, in a number of ways. Yet another example is the figure of the *orans*, or praying figure, which appears throughout early Christian art in both the paintings of the catacombs and the sculptures on sarcoph-agi. Its purpose is still being debated. Because of the hand gestures it has been linked with Noah and hence seen as another type of the resurrected Christ. Yet a brief look at the meaning of the words *orans* and *oratio* would suggest some-thing else.[14] To start with, *oratio* has two different meanings. In classical Latin the word means "speech"—hence our word *oration*—and an *orans* was anyone who spoke officially, for legal or even religious purposes. In Christian and medieval Latin the word means "prayer." Most dictionaries suggest that there is a clear distinction between the two uses of the word, but the usage of the early Church Fathers suggests something less absolute. While many of the Fathers (such as Hilary and Ambrose) use the word to mean "prayer" exclusively, some (such as Lactantius), use it in a Christian context to mean "rhetoric."[15] The two meanings are not as distinct as the dictionaries would imply. The two uses—and the two con-cepts involved—were, it would seem, linked to some degree.

Prayer may thus have been seen at first as a form of oration, maybe even specifically Christian oratory, and the *orans* can be understood not just as someone praying but also as someone orating. Given the definition of oration as used by Cicero and discussed in the first chapter, this seems a distinct possibility, if the inherent differences between the two forms of rhetoric are acknowledged. Directed at God, not man, prayer would perforce use different means than would classical oratory; faith, not reason, must rule, and so language, the tool of reason, must be supplemented by something else. While classical rhetoric attempts to persuade its audience through language, Christian prayer tries to convince through participation in faith.

In spite of these differences, however, both classical oration and Christian prayer are forms of communication that try to bring the audience closer to the speaker in their efforts at persuasion. The paintings in the catacombs illustrate even more clearly how the two processes can be the same, for here we have a situation in which Christians, through their art, are reminding their fellow Christians of their mutual faith. In a sense, their reminders are public oratory, much as sermons are, but they are also expressions of faith and as such are a form of prayer. They involve both reason and faith, both manipulation and participation. They differ from pagan oratory in insisting on the participation of the audience, which requires belief and prior acceptance. As both prayer and oratory the paintings show us prayer as oratory that has been adapted to Christian ends.

The *orans* figure serves as a reminder of the distinction between the two rhetorics. He appears in early Christian art as a signal or invitation to interpret. He is used, I would suggest, to insist that all paintings are to be treated as a combination of oratory and prayer and so to point out that the audience must not watch passively but must actively participate by interpreting. Sometimes the figure appears alone; at other times he is part of a scene, as in figure 3, a painting of Jonah from the catacomb of Petrus and Marcellinus where, interpolated into the narrative, he interrupts the story and inhibits the expected progress of plot. Instead of seeing the *orans* as a figure with a particular meaning, I would suggest that he is rather a metafigure whose purpose is to remind the audience to inter-

3. *Orans* and the story of Jonah. Catacomb of Petrus and Marcellinus (Lau E 3).

pret. He interrupts the story of Jonah much as the paralytic interrupted the picture of Adam and Eve, yet instead of suggesting a suitable fulfillment for the Old Testament story, the *orans* only suggests the presence, or possibility, of such a fulfillment. He is there to indicate that interpretation must take place; since he does not indicate what that interpretation or reading is, the actual discovery of truth is left up to the audience. His presence merely indicates that the audience must add something to the painting. He is reminding you to read scenes not as illustration but as symbol, in this case, as four separate and related symbols of death and resurrection. This is not just the story of Jonah; rather, it is both that story and something else, and the audience must figure out what that something else is.

A comparable rhetorical strategy can be found in a contemporary text, the apocryphal *Protevangelium of James*. Little has been written about the *Protevangelium* because its origin, date, and authorship remain largely unknown.[16] The focus of this tale is on Mary: the text includes a version of her birth and life, followed by a life of Christ. Several interesting anecdotes (such as the inclusion of the midwife) suggest its provenance, but for the most part it is an unremarkable account.

In the same way, the text moves, for the most part, in an expected, narrative fashion. Yet right at the moment of Christ's birth something extraordinary happens to the work. Because it is important to feel the anomalous nature of this moment I quote it in context:

> And they came into the middle of the road and Mary said to him: Take me down from off the ass, for that which is in me presses to come forth. And he took her down from off the ass and said to her: Whither shall I lead thee and cover thy disgrace for the place is desert. And he found a cave there, and led her into it; and leaving his two sons beside her he went out to seek a midwife in the district of Bethlehem.
> And I Joseph was walking and was not walking; and I looked up into the sky, and saw the sky astonished; and I

looked up to the pole of the heavens and saw it standing, and
the birds of the air keeping still. And I looked down upon
the earth and saw a trough lying, and work-people reclin-
ing: and their hands were in the trough. And those that were
eating did not eat, and those that were rising did not carry it
up, and those that were conveying anything to their mouths
did not convey it; but the faces of all were looking upwards.
And I saw the sheep walking, and the sheep stood still; and
the shepherd raised his hand to strike them, and his hand
remained up. And I looked upon the current of the river and
I saw the mouths of the kids resting on the water and not
drinking, and all things in a moment were driven from their
course.[17]

The clear break at the moment of Christ's birth is presented
in an unusual way: a shift in narrative voice and a shift in
narrative time both occur. The text breaks from a third-person
narrative that moves in time to a first-person witness account
("And I Joseph"; reminiscent in its way of the Book of
Revelation) that describes a situation in which time stands still.
On the simplest level, this strategy offsets Christ's birth. More
important for our purposes, however, there is a clear shift in
logic apparent here. Not only does the oratorical stance
change, but the narrative mode shifts from a discursive to a
tropic style, and consequently meaning becomes dependent on
a spatial, not a temporal, logic. The narrative that leads up to
this passage, in separating narrator from story, implies a
distinction between speaker and audience. When Joseph starts
to speak, however, the speaker and the audience converge, the
narrative is internalized, and instead of relating and controlling
the narrative, the speaker becomes a participating member of
the audience.

In addition to illustrating the orator's new role as participant,
the *Protevangelium* helps to explain further how this Christian
form of persuasion works and what it involves. For not only
does the narrative voice change at the moment of Christ's birth,
the events themselves shift into another mode. In each case
Joseph describes what he sees as something that is both hap-

pening and not happening. Each action is thus both itself and
not itself. This is a possible description of Christ, who is and
is not human, who is in time and not in time, and it is reminiscent in its particular formulation of the miracles—in every
instance, a miracle explores that moment at which a thing
becomes its defined other: making the blind man see means that
at least for the duration of the miracle the blind man's essence,
his blindness, is no longer true. What each miracle examines,
on one level, is a moment of linguistic paradox—here is the
blind man who is no longer blind. He is still the blind man—
that is his defining characteristic—and it was his blindness that
led to his being chosen; moreover, once the miracle has been
performed he remains the living proof of the power of Christ
precisely because he embodies a pair of opposites: he is blind and
not blind. Each of the miracles, I would suggest, creates such
a person who in his paradoxicality lives out an *imitatio Christi*:
in becoming his opposite he becomes like Christ.

Joseph's description of the events at Christ's birth are
similarly paradoxical. In the same way, we can picture a sheep
grazing and not grazing, eating and not eating. As with the
miracles, there are two possible ways of explicating these
scenes. The first is narratively—first the sheep graze and then
they don't. The second, more satisfactory reading of this
passage sees both of the contradictory events—eating and not
eating—as layers of an event occurring simultaneously. The
sheep are then grazing in one layer, not grazing in the next, as
the second action is laid over the first. In order to achieve
complete understanding we would have to see the two at the
same time, and read from one to the other. The second
member of each pair thus veils the first; only by reading the
two together does one, like Joseph, attain the full truth.

Significantly, the *orans* figure in the catacombs is frequently
shown with a veil. This could suggest the need for an
interpretation that unveils, like the one given the *Protevangelium* above. The best example of a veiled *orans* that functions in
this way is from the Velatio cubiculum in the catacomb of

Priscilla (fig. 4). The painting in question consists of three scenes; the problem lies in their interrelationship. While some feel that the figures are three representations of the same woman, presumably the deceased, shown at three crucial moments of her life (marriage, maternity, and death), I would suggest rather that the central figure be seen as the generic and metatextual veiled *orans* whose sole function is to suggest a relationship between the other two figures.[18] She is clearly meant to stand out: she faces the audience fully, is alone, and is much larger than the other figures. Moreover, because she is situated between the two other scenes—which are related to each other in their similar grouping of figures and their identical scale—she corresponds, in placement at least, to the other interpretative figures seen so far, the paralytic and the *orans*. Because the figure on the right bears a great resemblance to Nativity scenes, and because such Nativity scenes are frequently paired with either Old Testament prophetic scenes or the Fall, the figures to the left of the Velatio could represent Adam and Eve appearing before God in judgment and being sentenced to the life outside the garden. Together, these two scenes speak of the Fall and the Nativity—about death and birth—and, consequently, provide a statement about resurrection that is suitable for a burial spot. It is also possible, however, that the two figures in the scene on the left are males, as one seventeenth-century drawing would seem to suggest.[19] If so, then this scene could be identified as Cain and Abel bringing their offering to God, a scene repeated in other catacombs. This, too, would pair nicely with the Madonna and child: fruits of the Fall, fruit of the womb. In either reading, the role of the central figure remains the same: she is there to prod the audience into making a connection and to suggest the veiled quality of the truth of the painting,[20] or, as Clement of Alexandria put it, to suggest that "all things that shine through a veil show the truth grander and more imposing; as fruits shining through water, and figures through

4. Veiled *orans*. Catacomb of Priscilla (Pri L 5).

veils which give added reflections to them. . . . Since then we may draw several meanings as we do from what is expressed in veiled form, . . . the ignorant and unlearned man fails."[21]

Perhaps the best example of all, which will take us back to Augustine, is a series of paintings, ranging from the second to fourth centuries, all of which depict the story of the three boys in the fire from the Book of Daniel.[22] The scene can and has been explained as a type of the Resurrection: thrown into the fire for refusing to worship the idol of Nabuchodnosor, the three boys (Sidrach, Misach, and Abednago) are miraculously saved. Yet there is more to this scene, particularly if we look at a series of examples of the painting in comparison with the following passage from Daniel:

> Then Nabuchodnosor the king was astonished and rose up in haste and said to his nobles: Did we not cast three men bound into the midst of the fire? They answered the king and said: True o king.
>
> He answered and said Behold I see four men loose and walking in the midst of the fire. And there is no hurt in them: and the form of the fourth is like the Son of God.
>
> Then Nabuchodnosor came to the door of the burning fiery furnace and said: Sidrach, Misach and Abednago, ye servants of the most high God, go ye forth, and come. And immediately Sidrach, Misach, and Abednago went out from the midst of the fire. (*Dan.* 3.91–93; Douay-Confraternity translation)

Of particular interest in turning from the text to its illustration in the catacomb is whether the painter chose to depict the fourth figure or not, for what the scene represents in addition to resurrection is enlightenment. Nabuchodnosor sees something that he has not seen before and that no one else can see just then, and he is persuaded by the truth of this vision to let the three boys go. When you paint this scene do you show the vision or not? Should you, in other words, allow the audience to have the experience Nabuchodnosor had and not paint the fourth figure, or do you make the painting spell out the letter of the text and paint the fourth boy?

The answer to this question changes, and that shift is telling. In the early depictions of this scene, for the most part, the three boys are shown alone. Often the presence of the fourth figure is only implied by the gaze of the three figures. In later fourth-century versions of this scene, however, the fourth figure is inserted, either literally or symbolically—for example, figure 5, from the cubiculum of the Velatio, in which the fourth figure is implied by the presence of the raven; or figure 6, from the *Coemeterium Maius*, in which he is represented by the hand of God.

The shift in the iconography of this scene reflects a change in most Christian art and rhetoric of the fourth century. In the later versions of this scene the fourth figure is depicted, thus essentially denying the possibility of participation on the part of the audience. Where the earlier examples leave room for interpretation, later examples do not. The later versions seem, as these examples suggest, to illustrate rather than involve. Their purpose seems more decorative than doctrinal, and their rhetoric more classical than Christian.[23]

The Divine Spark

The assumptions that guided the artistic choices made by the catacomb painters are comparable to those of Augustine. His works can be seen as an apologia for the pure, true, earlier Christian style, a uniquely Christian form of persuasion that will communicate by its structure as much as by its content the fundamental tenets of Christianity—Christian truths communicated in a Christian way. Just what that way is, however, has yet to be determined here: Augustine, as usual, offers a series of responses and models to which we will now turn.

Through Christian artists such as the catacomb painters,

5. Three boys in the furnace with raven. Catacomb of Priscilla (Pri L 12).

6. Three boys in the furnace with hand of God. *Coemeterium Maius* (Mag D 25).

rhetoric—Cicero's rhetoric of speaking well to persuade—
becomes a hermeneutics, and even as the pragmatics shifted, so
the mechanics of active persuasion likewise changed. If and
when Christian man assumes the role of persuader—as of
course he must often do—the ways and means open to him
will differ from those prescribed by classical rhetoric. Instead
of insisting on the absolute power and verity of language and
reason, the Christian persuader must remain part of the
audience even while assuming temporarily what is objectively
the role of teacher. There is consequently a reorganization of
the hierarchy implicit in classical rhetoric, for no matter how
much the Christian teacher or preacher is like the classical
orator, he is also like the Ciceronian audience. Such power as
the classical orator has over his audience—a power possible
only if a distance exists between them—is thus denied.[24]
Moreover, the audience, who, at least theoretically, had no
voice, now has, at least in part, the voice of the orator, since
the orator is always part of the audience. The shift in pragmatics is thus a shift in underlying assumptions: the Christian
orator must persuade laterally, not from on high, and all that
he says is subject to a higher authority.

Augustine discusses this shift in authority in many of his
works, of which we will consider only a handful. In his text *De
magistro* he introduces this theme by insisting on the ultimate
impossibility of communicating through language.[25] While
seeming to provide a powerful invective against the ability of
men to relate to God and an assertion of their ultimate inability
to communicate, it is, in the end, a vehement assertion of the
bond that unites them. For while we do indeed not know what
a given sign means to our audience, this does not mean that we
cannot communicate. We merely cannot explain how we
communicate. The analogy implicit here is that of the relationship between man and God, which, though incommunicable
and rationally inexplicable, is nonetheless possible. But this
does not mean that we cannot know God. It means, rather,
that our knowledge of God remains a mystery, that the

relation between God and man is like that of signifier and signified—there and not there at the same time. The fact that we cannot explain the precise nature of the relationship does not deny its existence; rather, at least in a sacred context, it asserts it. All it denies is our ability to reduce that relationship to rational terms, and as such stands as a strong statement in favor of the ultimate transcendence of God.[26]

In the *Confessions* we find a comparable argument for this shift in rhetorical focus. Most important in this regard are the scenes of stealing from the pear tree, the conversion in the garden, and the conversation between Augustine and his mother in Ostia. While each has been written on extensively, I wish to focus on their essentially oratorical nature in order to discuss their rhetorical and allusive underpinnings.[27] Moreover, I wish to see them as a sort of typological triptych. While it is usually the Resurrection that is paired with the Fall—the wood of the cross taken from the tree of knowledge—Augustine quite clearly through the setting and layout of the conversion scene shows the Annunciation as the answer to and redemption of the Fall.

The parallel between the stealing of the pears and Eve's taking of the apple is clear: seduced by another, Augustine takes the pears not to eat but just to have sinned:

> arbor erat pirus in vicinia nostrae vineae pomis onusta nec forma nec sapore inlecebrosis. ad hanc excutiendam atque asportandam nequissimi adulescentuli perreximus nocte intempesta, quo usque ludum de pestilentiae more in areis produxeramus, et abstulimus inde onera ingentia non ad nostras epulas, sed vel proicienda porcis, etiamsi aliquid inde comedimus, dum tamen fieret a nobis quod eo liberet, quo non liceret. (2.4)

> There was a pear-tree near our vineyard, loaded with fruit that was attractive neither to look nor to taste. Late one night a band of ruffians, myself included, went off to shake down the fruit and carry it away. . . .We took an enormous quantity of pears, not to eat them ourselves, but simply to

throw them to the pigs. Perhaps we ate some of them, but our real pleasure lay in doing something that was forbidden.[28]

There is little indication that Augustine is acting of his own accord. Rather, he appears to be capitulating to peer pressure; he does it because the others suggested it. Also, he steals because of the power the outcome promises to provide: having stolen the pears, he and his comrades will have the added satisfaction of knowing they had flouted the rules of their society. So Eve, promised power if she eats the apple, and knowing that tree to be the one she is not to touch, follows the advice of the serpent.

While the persuasive aspect is implicit in this scene, it is reinforced by the explicit rhetorical cast given Augustine's conversion.[29] Set in a garden, it includes also a conversation. Significantly, though, a storm of tears precedes that conversation, a storm that Augustine both dwells upon and gives in to:

> Ubi vero a fundo arcano alta consideratio traxit et congessit totam miseriam meam in conspectu cordis mei, oborta est procella ingens ferens ingentem imbrem lacrimarum. (8.12)

> I probed the hidden depths of my soul and wrung its pitiful secrets from it, and when I mustered them all before the eyes of my heart, a great storm broke within me, bringing with it a great deluge of tears.[30]

Instead of calming the storm like the orator Neptune does in the first book of the *Aeneid*, or as Cicero suggests in the *De inventione*, Augustine finally gives in to these feelings.[31] Torn apart by doubt and desire Augustine, flinging himself beneath a fig tree, questions God. As if in response he hears:

> cum cantu dicentis et crebro repetentis quasi pueri an puellae, nescio: "tolle lege, tolle lege." statimque mutato vultu intentissimus cogitare coepi, utrumnam solerent pueri in aliquo genere ludendi cantitare tale aliquid, nec occurrebat omnino audisse me uspiam repressoque impetu lacrimarum surrexi nihil aliud interpretans divinitus mihi iuberi, nisi ut

aperirem codicem et legerem quod primum caput invenissem. (8.12)

the sing-song voice of a child in a nearby house. Whether it was the voice of a boy or girl I cannot say, but again and again it repeated the refrain "Take it and read, take it and read." At this I looked up, thinking hard whether there was any kind of game in which children used to chant words like these, but I could not remember ever hearing them before. I stemmed my flood of tears and stood up, telling myself that this could only be a divine command to open my book of Scripture and read the first passage on which my eyes should fall.[32]

The children's advice to go and read does not have the direct seductive effect that the serpent's has on Eve or that of Augustine's friends has on him.[33] Instead, he hesitates, then turns back to Alypius, where, opening the Bible at random, he reads the first text he comes to. The pear is replaced, quite literally, by the Word; with echoes of the Eucharist in the background, Augustine takes in the Scriptures—embodies and incarnates the Word—instead of ingesting the pear.[34] Two important insights surface from this comparison: First, Augustine does not just follow blindly the advice of the children. He turns back of his own free will and in that turning is converted. Second, the entire process is shown to be rhetorical: he is told by children's voices; he is saved by words. But the strategies and pragmatics are fundamentally different from those of the Fall. Instead of following advice like Eve—an action reminiscent of Cicero's method of persuasion—he hesitates before accepting, and he interprets what he reads. These two seemingly unrelated actions are in fact manifestations of a single process that comprises an essential characteristic of Christian persuasion. Actively participating, either by answering the voices in returning to his friend or by answering the text with exegesis, marks something new and essential: an introduction of will and dialogue. Christian rhetoric, at least in this case, seems to require the interaction between speaker and audience—a question-and-answer dialogue—that implies the willing and necessary participation of the audience in the process of attaining the truth.

Augustine's conversion in the garden is also a conversion of his role and relation with language. He moves from being an orator, or vendor of words, to being an *orans* or, person who prays, and he develops from being a signmaker, as he is at the start of his non-Christian, preconversion life, to a sign reader, as he becomes at the end: not only does his actual conversion include reading, but the remainder of the text—almost exactly half its overall length—consists of meditations on discrete topics and long interpretative passages.[35]

Marcia Colish, in her extraordinary book *The Mirror of Language*, suggests that Augustine's rhetoric is, from this moment on, incarnational.[36] I would agree and, more, would suggest that the Annunciation provides not only the context for understanding Augustine's conversion but also a matrix by which we can make sense of Christian persuasion in general and its difference from classical rhetoric. The Annunciation as the conception of the Word is a logical starting point for understanding Christian rhetoric; it stands to the Christian system as Cicero's etiological myth of suppression stands to his. And as in the case of Cicero, it is important to see what the presuppositions of such a scene are.

Luke and other early Christian accounts of the Annunciation emphasize dialogue and participation. Unlike Eve, Mary hesitates, asking, "Why me?" and then announces her willingness to be the *ancilla domini*, and hence to participate.[37] And it is at that moment—at her accepting of the covenant—that Christ is conceived.

Moreover, the standard iconography of the Annunciation freezes the moment of hesitation and thus emphasizes its importance. So, for example, the earliest extant Annunciation, in the second-century catacomb of Priscilla, uses a standard iconography of oration, the *adlocutio* topos, to depict the relationship between the two characters (fig. 7). It is clearly

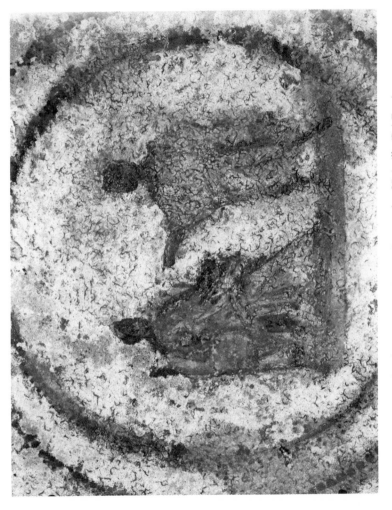

7. Gabriel appearing to Mary. Catacomb of Priscilla (Pri E 30).

seen as a rhetorical moment, and even in this very early depiction there is an ambivalence over which of the characters is the orator, which has the power: is it Mary, who, as seated figure, is iconographically compared to God, or is she merely the audience to Gabriel, who, in his *adlocutio* pose, is likewise comparable to an orator? Later on, the standard iconography of the Annunciation projects a similar ambivalence, as Gabriel is shown kneeling, Mary hesitating; each with power, yet each humble; both deferring to some higher authority.

The transformation in the *Confessions* of the garden scene from one patterned on Eve and the devil to one patterned on Mary and Gabriel has far-reaching ramifications. Whereas the interaction between the devil and Eve suggests that by eating the apple, by acknowledging, accepting, and acting on the devil's words, Eve can herself become a powerful figure, that is, not only like God but like the devil himself; Gabriel and Mary's interaction, as well as the phrasing of her acceptance (*ecce ancilla domini*), suggest a new hierarchy.[38] Mary as handmaiden posits, and insists upon, the superiority of her Lord. She is and will remain the audience. Yet while this relation may seem more oppressive in its rigidity, it is, in the end, at least theoretically more liberating. For while the classical rhetorical model insists upon the constant suppression of one group by another with language as the weapon of that struggle, the annunciatory model, though it insists similarly on a speaker and an audience, allows for a greater parity between them. Even though Mary is God's handmaiden, the difference in rank is not—theoretically—a means to suppression; even though as handmaiden she holds a position comparable to that of Juno, inferiority of rank here is not equated with loss of voice. Her lower, humbled position is seen as a privilege, and rhetoric tranforms to support it.

Concomitant with this change is an increase in the participation and power of the audience. The expression of will demonstrated by Mary's hesitation and acceptance of God's offer is central here, for it implies that her status as handmaiden is not one of subjection. She willingly enters into the contract; she starts what eventually becomes a continuous dialogue with God. She is a handmaiden because she answers, not because she submits.

Through the Annunciation man becomes the permanent audience to God's orations. He also becomes the answerer to questions posed. His role is thus fixed, and hence language, too, becomes fixed. It retains its central status as the defining signifying system, yet even as the order of power shifts, so language and its function change. Language becomes the model, not the means of attaining truth. Behind the Annunciation lies the assumption that the creation of the Word—as both God and man, eternal and temporal, signified and signifer—meant the creation of a relationship between God and man. That relationship was characterized both by man's acceptance of his permanent role as audience—albeit active and participatory—and by the fact that through language one can approach God and truth. Yet as permanent audience, language is now directed and used in a different way. Instead of being used to convince other men of the truths achieved and conceived through the rational powers language has given us, language now becomes a means for pursuing the higher, and eminently nonrational, truths of God. As audience we need convince no one but ourselves; as active participants we need to follow out those possibilities that language offers to us, but those possibilities are now aimed in a different direction. All language is one Word; all life is now aimed at understanding that Word. Whatever persuading we do—of fellow believers or nonbelievers—will be aimed at explaining the meaning of the Word.

In the shift from Eve to Mary, from language as a transferable commodity to language as a fixed relationship between man and God, rhetoric likewise undergoes a conversion. While Eve's transaction with the serpent and then with Adam can be seen as rhetorical, Mary's conversation with Gabriel is more of a hermeneutical act. Eve is a sign maker dealing in the realm of the sole signifier, Mary a sign reader pursuing an implied relation between the signifier and the ultimate signified. While both involve persuasion, the one insists on using language toward an end, the other on making and accepting a participatory role in a fixed and established relationship.

I would therefore suggest that Augustine's "conversion" in the garden is not the moment of complete transformation. It is all too easily commented on, analyzed, and explained to provoke any real response from the audience. Moreover, the reader has just experienced, albeit from more of a distance, the conversion of Victorinus, a conversion that is for all intents and purposes identical to—and consequently adumbrates—that of Augustine.

The problem with this conversion scene, in fact, is that there is no conversion. Nothing happens that has not happened before; no revelation occurs that cannot be explained fully in language. Such interpretation as occurs here consists largely of setting the conversion scene in a completely verbal context of Scripture and of preceding conversions, which then serves to explain Augustine's conversion.

I would suggest that this is the scene most commented on because it conforms most closely to the old ways of rhetoric, not the new. It is the scene that we are awaiting from page one, the moment Augustine is building toward—narratively, rhetorically—throughout the text. It has provoked the most critical comment because it fulfills all of the audience's expectations. Everything tells us to react to it as pivotal—theme, plot, even structural repetition. Yet this kind of narrative programming has less to do with incarnational rhetoric than with classical. We read the passage the way we look at a Pompeian painting, not a catacomb fresco. We do not actively participate; instead, we are led through and told what to do and how to think at every stage.

One could argue at this point that it is virtually impossible to write without clues of this sort. I would suggest that if Christian rhetoric offers anything new it is precisely the possibility that such manipulation need not—in fact, must not—occur if one is to experience the sublime. When one is led through a scene, its mystery is dispelled. As soon as one escapes—as soon as one feels one is allowed to choose, to decide, and not merely to identify and supply answers, to participate and not merely to react—then mystery becomes once again possible.

Augustine offers us such a scene in the *Confessions*. The true scene of his conversion is, I would suggest, the neo-Platonic sublime passage from book 9 in which he talks with his mother. Not only are we not told what they said to each other (the conversation is paraphrased), but the vision is left incomplete and the chapter ends abruptly, without gloss of any sort. Until recently, critics have chosen to downplay the importance of this scene. One who hasn't, Eugene Vance, treats the two scenes as a pair, and after commenting in detail on the impact and meaning of the garden scene, he ends his article with a lengthy quotation of the passage from book 9.[39]

Vance's tacit reading of this scene is exactly what it should be: the open-ended silence that allows for audience participation. Augustine offers us not one but two conversion scenes, two turning points in the text, one of which is programmed and virtually explained, one of which is left shrouded in mystery. His conversion is thus twofold, and, by extension, we feel that Christian rhetoric in general must likewise have two parts: that of a Ciceronian orator, who keeps his narrative unities of time and place intact and projects his own voice into the lead characters, and that of the Augustine who is "converted" by his mother and her death in Ostia. This narrative takes over after the conversion and moves into a reading of Genesis. This is the truly new text, the text that reads, interprets, and leaves meaning up in the air.[40]

Notice also how the scene compares in its visual composition to several scenes in the *Aeneid*. Augustine is talking to his mother, entreating; so Venus in book 1 of the *Aeneid* appeals to Jupiter for advice and help. Yet in the *Confessions* both

Augustine and his mother are ultimately audience to an even higher power—God's words. Like Mary, Monica is the focus of the scene; she both is deferred to and ultimately defers, to a higher, more silent authority.

Moreover, this scene takes place at a window, inside a house, and thus is visually comparable to the iconography of the Annunciation both in the arrangement of the characters involved and in the setting in which they are placed. Its emblematic aspect is thus very telling and important as it rewrites several scenes from the *Aeneid* and earlier in the *Confessions* in a way that calls the Annunciation to mind. By placing Monica on a level with—if not in some ways superior to—her son, Augustine suggests a hierarchical rearrangement of the classical relation of speaker to audience, as well as of male to female.

But the Annunciation has further significance, for as the Word is made flesh, the verbal accedes to the visual and the two are joined in dialogue. Consequently, if we, like Mary, see ourselves as readers—as Mary figures—then every true reading we give will involve the embodiment of word into the nonverbal. This is best explored in the arts by a shift in discipline from language to vision. As we read we envision; every act of reading involves an incarnation and passes from words to things, from the verbal to the nonverbal. As the word becomes the thing—be it vision or idea—the gap between the two is bridged without being bridged. In crossing from one discipline to another, the reader thus experiences Christ or understands in ways that transcend reason and language. This crossing is organized not according to a discursive, narrative logic but, rather, by a nonnarrative order, an order of charity, not fear; love not logic,[41] and while this statement refers on one level to the organization of Augustine's text, it implies the intellectual process that must take place if understanding through this new rhetoric is to occur. This order of love is, judging from the organization of the *Confessions*, hardly an order at all—at times the text seems structured around nothing more systematic than free association. Yet this can also be viewed as a tropic order: issues are ordered by figures of speech, not by discursive logic. A series of turnings, of tropings, underlies the narrative order of Augustine's plot and reflects a projection of the tropic order implied in reading such a text. The reader must read and read into such a text, even as Augustine reads and reads into other texts. Succession is often that of priority, not time, and the links between sections—paragraphs and chapters—are similarly spatialized.

This spatiality is important, as it implies a monumentality to Augustine's text that is often ignored. Such a concrete approach to the word is implied by the concept of the Word made flesh. Even as much of the unique style of Augustine's works comes from their metaphoricity, both in style and order, so this metaphoricity adds a spatial dimension to the text that enables it to rehearse the Incarnation: it is truly a word made thing.

Moreover, if understanding takes place at the juncture of these two modes—between words and things, between language and vision, between the order of reason giving way to the order of love—then the means by which sense is achieved and communicated lies in the part of the trope that cannot be troped; the point where word becomes thing is where creation and understanding take place. While sometimes that point is represented as silence or a gap, artists often show it in some way, offering it at least a means of identification. So in later medieval depictions of the Annunciation, the visual focus is displaced from either character to the space between them. In the earlier versions that use this iconography something interrupts the visual plane directly between them, be it a column, the wall of the house, a flower; in later versions that area is opened out by a window or an arch, yet attention remains riveted to that spot as it becomes the vanishing point for the perspective. This iconography both suggests a shift in power from Mary and Gabriel to some higher authority and offers the added possibility that the higher authority cannot be depicted, nor the process of understanding charted in any analyzable or reproducible way. The process of persuasion that takes place between Gabriel and Mary—that process which is ritualistically repeated in every act of Christian rhetoric—consists of a dialogue, a question and answer, and a third element without which that dialogue cannot take place. That third element, the divine element, is both temporal and atemporal. Similarly, in a visual, spatial medium, it is the point at which everything comes together, visually, while also representing the point where nothing actually converges.

While the Annunciation does, indeed, provide a pragmatic model for Christian rhetoric that shows graphically, as we have seen, the restructuring of power involved, the development of the model is Augustine's own. There is, however, a second model, derived ultimately from Plato, that Christian authors and artists before and including Augustine had used: the concept of the divine spark.

In the *De catechizandis rudibus*, Augustine explains to a friend how to persuade the nonbeliever. The *De catechizandis* is in many respects a rewriting of the earlier *De magistro*, where, as we have seen, Augustine undertakes a similar task, to explain to his son how teaching occurs and whether understanding ever truly happens. In the *De catechizandis*, however, still acknowledging that truth resides beyond rational discourse, Augustine asserts its access by offering a description of how such knowledge is obtained.[42] In other words, instead of leaving open the question of entry into the ineffable, and the means unexplained, Augustine details the mechanics of such a mode of communication:

> Totum enim quod intelligo, volo ut qui me audit intelligat; et sentio me non ita loqui, ut hoc efficiam: maxime quia ille intellectus quasi rapida coruscatione perfundit animum. . . . Quapropter coniciendum est quantum distet sonus oris nostri ab illo ictu intelligentiae, quando ne ipsi quidem impressioni memoriae similis est.[43]

All that I indeed understand I want he who hears me to

understand; and I feel that I am not speaking so that this may happen: mostly because that understanding pierces the mind like a rapid spark. . . .Because of that, the degree to which the sound of my mouth differs from that moment of understanding must be conjectured, since it is not like the trace left by memory.

The words Augustine uses to describe this process of communication are notable for two reasons: first, for their use of metaphor, and second, for their literary and philosophical tradition. The passage, far from being original with Augustine, is a paraphrase of a passage from the Seventh Letter, assumed at the time to be written by Plato.[44] As we shall see shortly, where it is not quoted it is paraphrased, where it is not paraphrased its logic is assumed into the structure of texts that discuss or demonstrate this phenomenon. In short, it permeates Christian literature preceding and including Augustine that confronts the question of persuasion.

The Seventh Letter explains that not everyone is fit to study philosophy. In order to separate the true philosophers from those not cut out for the task, the following method is proposed: "demonstrate to such people the nature of the subject as a whole, and all the stages that must be gone through, and how much labour is required. If the hearer has the divine spark which makes philosophy congenial to him and fits him for its pursuit, the way described to him appears so wonderful that he must follow it with all his might if life is to be worth living." In a similar manner, the text suggests that knowledge itself cannot be explained directly or rationally: "in my judgment it is impossible that ⟨any⟩ should have understanding of the subject. No treatise by me concerning it exists or ever will exist. It is not something that can be put into words like other branches of learning; only after a long partnership in a common life devoted to this very thing does truth flash upon the soul, like a flame kindled by a leaping spark."[45]

What the passage from the Seventh Letter implies is that

truth is beyond teaching, beyond words. While words can lead to the threshold of knowledge, beyond that, language is to no avail—truth must come to the audience "like a flame kindled by a leaping spark." That we still have a similar metaphor for intuitive understanding—be it the flash of understanding, or even the lowly light bulb of cartoons—seems to indicate that this metaphor is not chosen arbitrarily. For the metaphor—as used, for example, by Augustine—suggests that all Christian communication, particularly to the unconverted (but also, as we shall see, to the converted), will flash upon the soul and that every word will ultimately give way to or transform into a visual image.[46]

The thrust of this simile is to suggest that words, because of their sanctified status and relation to the ineffable, will take as the ultimate reality a nonverbal, atemporal form, that final understanding will occur as word becomes thing, as verbal becomes nonverbal, in the moment of crossing between the two.[47]

This understanding of the passage from the Seventh Letter is supported by its use in the Christian tradition that precedes and prepares the way for Augustine. Other neo-Platonists had seized upon it and crowded its understanding with biblical resonances. Porphyry, for instance, quotes it in *On Parmenides* 10; Plotinus refers to it in *Soliloquy* 2.2.34; Origen in *Contra Celsum* 6.3. The most striking example of all, however, links this model directly with the catacomb paintings by means of a painting found in the Via Latina catacomb. This catacomb, discovered in 1954, contains the highest density of paintings of any of the catacombs, executed in several different periods.[48] The scene I wish to discuss (fig. 8) is found in cubiculum A, together with other common catacomb scenes such as Adam and Eve, Susanna and the elders, and the Good Shepherd. For a long time this scene was labeled as the Sermon on the Mount,[49] yet when the painting is compared to that event in Matthew the identification clearly does not hold true. Matthew states specifically that after Christ went up on the moun-

8. Moses on Mount Sinai. Via Latina Catacomb (Din A 3).

tain "his disciples came to him." Though this painting is badly
preserved, it is still possible to see that this speaker is not
surrounded by his followers. Rather, he is distinctly removed
from them. The organization of the painting conforms, in fact,
rather closely to one version of a common topos of speaker and
crowd, the *adlocutio* topos, where the speaker stands raised and
to the right of his audience. This topos might well have been
known to the painter of this scene, as it was depicted on coins
from the first and second centuries.[50] There is, however, one
significant difference between the arrangement here and the
pagan *adlocutio*. All the pagan *adlocutiones* connect the speaker
with his audience by means of a continuous groundline, suggestive, perhaps, of the continuity Cicero tries to establish
through his rhetoric between himself and his audience. The
speaker appears to be in his own space, completely separated
from the crowd below. As if to emphasize this fact, the crowd
is turned away from him and faces us instead. It seems likely,
then, that this scene should be identified, as others have con-
tended, not as the Sermon on the Mount but as Moses on Mount
Sinai, where the text clearly supports the iconography of the
painting: "Be ready in the morning that thou mayst forthwith
go up unto Mt. Sinae: and thou shalt stand with me upon the
top of the Mount. Let no man go up with thee: and let not any
man be seen throughout all the Mount." And further: ". . . and
Aaron and the children of Israel, seeing the face of Moses
horned, were afraid to come near" (Exod. 34.2-3, 30; Douay-
Confraternity). But how do we read this painting? As we have
noted, most of the Old Testament scenes in the catacombs can
be explained typologically; most are painted in such a way as
to remind the audience of their typological pair. Yet here that
possibility seems to have been deliberately denied. Instead of
emphasizing the connection between Moses on Mount Sinai
and Christ on the Mount, the painter has remained faithful to
the text in a way that denies a typological reading. This is an
illustration of the scene from Exodus and nothing else. So why
include it?

First, a stylistic approach will give us a partial answer. There is, as I mentioned, a space between the speaker and his audience, which conforms to the Scripture even as it breaks with the traditional depiction of this topos. Yet if the conventional pagan iconography is meant to reflect the common power of speech, then perhaps the break in groundline indicates that speech alone is not sufficient for such an oration. Perhaps it even suggests that there is no common bond between speaker and audience and that something more than speech is required for this communication. Perhaps Moses is portrayed on a different plane from the crowd below because he now possesses divine knowledge, and thus is closer to God, but cannot communicate it fully to his audience. Perhaps the artist paints him on a detached and raised level in order to indicate his divine powers, which are not completely translatable.

Clement of Alexandria, in his discussion of this passage from Exodus, provides a key:

> For it is both a difficult task to discover the Father and Maker of this universe; and having found him it is impossible to declare Him to all. For this is by no means capable of expression like the other subjects of instruction, says the truth-loving Plato. For he had heard right well that the all-wise Moses, ascending the Mount for holy contemplation, to the summit of intellectual objects, necessarily commands that the whole people do not accompany him. And when the Scripture says, "Moses entered into the thick darkness where God was," this shows to those capable of understanding that God is invisible and beyond expression by words. And "the darkness" which is, in truth, the unbelief and ignorance of the multitude—obstructs the gleam of truth.[51]

The Via Latina painting is no more an illustration of the scriptural text than Clement's passage is an objective description of it. Both interpret the Scriptures and both offer similar readings of the text. The gap in the catacomb painting corresponds to the thick darkness described in Clement's

exegesis. Both the fourth-century painter and the second-
century exegete see in this passage an attempt by man to
communicate God's truth to man. Each of them shows this in
a similar way: we can see in each interpretation an emblematic
representation of the process of Christian *oratio*. Direct communication of the divine truth through any rational medium is
not possible. It must instead involve the participation of the
audience before the complete truth is obtained; the truth must
flash upon the soul like a flame kindled by a leaping spark.

Given the constant recurrence of the passage from the
Seventh Letter and its consistent interpretation and understanding, it seems possible that such a model was in fact
implicit in, or subsumed by, most understandings of Christian
communication; that while the Annunciation provided the
pragmatic verbal model, the Seventh Letter offered the visual,
rhetorical one. The two complement each other in their
insistence on the limitations of language and reason and their
focus on the transformation of word into object.

The *De doctrina christiana* and the Doctrine of *De inveniendo*

The best prescriptive description of Augustine's rhetoric, as
well as the most elaborate discussion of its full potential, is
provided in the *De doctrina christiana*. This text has been studied
in many ways, most recently as a guide to Christian culture.[52]
It is also, however, a guide to the transformation of rhetoric.
The first book begins:

> Duae sunt res quibus nititur omnis tractatio scripturarum,
> modus inveniendi quae intellegenda sunt et modus profe-
> rendi quae intellecta sunt. De inveniendo prius, de profe-
> rendo postea disseremus.

> There are two things necessary to the treatment of the
> Scriptures: a way of discovering things which are to be

understood, and a way of teaching what we have learned. We shall speak first of discovery and second of teaching.[53]

The translation is that of D. W. Robertson, and while his renditions of *inveniendo* and *proferendo* as "discovering" and "teaching" are literally accurate, they do not fully convey certain resonances of these two key terms. Both of these words are variations of technical rhetorical terms: *inveniendo* is a form of *invenire*, the first of five divisions in Ciceronian rhetoric; *proferendo* the gerund form of a synonym for *pronuntiatio*, the last division.[54] Augustine is suggesting by his use and adaptation of these terms that his text is a rewriting of classical rhetoric—a rewriting that will allow classical oratory to incorporate and communicate the new truths and enable it once again to be a useful social tool.[55] In the following pages I will argue that the *De doctrina christiana* provides us with a model for the communication of all textual truths—profane as well as sublime—throughout the Middle Ages.[56]

Like that of Cicero, Augustine's real interest lay with the first of these divisions. Cicero's proposed five-part work (one on each division) never got beyond the *De inventione*;[57] Augustine's first draft of the *De doctrina christiana* likewise covered only the *de inveniendo*.[58] Only later did he add the now unduly famous fourth book on teaching. Within the *de inveniendo* Augustine focused on one particular problem: how to deal with parts of the Scriptures that are ambiguous or obscure. While he does mention other aspects of the Scriptures, his real concern is with what is clearly most important: how properly to treat the parts of the Scriptures that do not in and of themselves speak well of God.[59] These are the places that, for obvious reasons, are most in need of controlled interpretation, the places where the mechanics of the *de inveniendo* can be most fruitfully applied.

What does it mean, *de inveniendo*? In the preface to the *De doctrina christiana* Augustine states that "he who receives the precepts we wish to teach will not need another to reveal those things which need explaining when he finds [*invenerit*] any obscurity in books. . . . But by following certain traces [*vestigiis*] he may come to the hidden sense without any error. . . ."[60] The role of the well-trained reader, then, is to ferret out those spots where the text is ambiguous or obscure and then, *quibusdam vestigiis indagatis*, come to the proper meaning. *De inveniendo* is thus the process of locating the difficult spots in the Scriptures and then turning onto the proper path indicated by the traces or footprints of the proper reading. The ambulatory metaphor implied by *vestigiis* is reinforced by the final line of the preface, the "proper beginning for the road we wished to follow" ("huius viae quam in hoc libro ingredi volumus, tale nobis occurrit exordium"),[61] a metaphor that leads us, in turn, to a better understanding of this process of reading. We are, Augustine says, to find in the text traces of what was, traces of other meanings that reside outside or beyond the surface of the text, footprints on roads that lead from the literal, ambiguous level of meaning. This image of the road or way is not gratuitous. Rather, it is used throughout the *De doctrina christiana* in reference to a complex of readings that are to be seen as comparable: that of the *De doctrina christiana* itself, that of the Scriptures, and that of Christ, the Word made flesh.[62] In the passage in which Augustine relates Christ to the way, we are offered a fuller picture of how we are to understand and use the *vestigia* of ambiguous signs. We move closer to Christ, we are told, by means of the way, but also—and this is significant—by means of Christ, who is himself the way: "Sic enim ait: Ego sum via et veritas et vita, hoc est, per me venitur, ad me pervenitur, in me permanetur. . . . via nostra esse dignatus est" ("Thus He says: 'I am the way, and the truth, and the life'; that is, you are to come through me, to arrive at me, and to remain in me. . . . He saw fit to become our road").[63] Christ and the way are thus both means and end, process and goal. Through him we achieve him and, it is implied, attain truth. Thus the process of moving from the ambiguous sign to its proper meaning is as important— as full of truth—as the actual achievement of understanding; in the moving from the obscure to the true one has found the truth.

This understanding of *de inveniendo* as process supplemented by end is supported by Augustine's definition of charity.[64] In the passage made famous by D. W. Robertson's reliance upon it in *A Preface to Chaucer*, Augustine defines charity as the sole message of the Scriptures. In Robertson's translation: "Scripture teaches nothing but charity, nor condemns anything except cupidity . . .";[65] Robertson glosses this with an earlier line: "whatever appears in the divine Word that does not literally pertain to virtuous behaviour or the truth of faith you must take to be figurative. . . ." He adds: "A discipline is thus afforded for the exegete. Those passages which promote charity or condemn cupidity are to be left with their literal significance; but all figurative interpretations must promote the love of God and of one's neighbor." [66] Yet this gloss does not completely correspond to Augustine's own gloss of the process. The line quoted above ends "et eo modo informat mores hominum" ("and in this way shapes the minds of men").[67] This informing process comes about through charity itself, it is implied, for charity, Augustine tells us, is "motum animi ad fruendum deo propter ipsum et se atque proximo propter deum" ("the motion of the soul toward the enjoyment of God for His own sake, and the enjoyment of one's self and of one's neighbor for the sake of God").[68] Charity is thus not only, as Robertson would have it, the static message of the Scriptures. It is also the process of moving toward God, and as such it is exactly parallel to Augustine's understanding of Christ, who is both the end of the road and the road itself. In its duality charity thus corresponds also to the process of reading and interpreting. In finding an obscure or ambiguous (read: cupidinous) spot in the Scriptures, we experience charity as we turn from the literal cupidinous reading to the implied higher charitable meaning. In the turning, in the movement itself, lies the way to salvation; salvation begins *in principio viarum*.

I would suggest that what Augustine is positing in his *de inveniendo* is a hermeneutics of charity, that from reading Scripture we learn the message and process of charity. I will go even further and propose that the message of charity is important only as a means of defining the extent of the process. As we have seen, this dual function is exactly parallel to our experience of Christ, who is likewise means to an end. In both cases, however, there is an implied rift between the journey and the arrival, between knowing and approaching the goal of charity, on the one hand, and actually achieving that end, on the other. Through Christ we know our God and thus define our goal; so in reading we posit our charitable reading above our cupidinous one and in so doing move from one pole to the other. But the power of reading, like the power of Christ, derives from the fact that we never lose sight of our point of origin. Rather, we hover in our reading, as in life, between the two, experiencing the rift even as we gloss over it. This, I would suggest, is what Augustine is referring to when he asserts, at the start of the *De doctrina christiana*, that one cannot understand the obscurities of the Scriptures without the particular precepts he is about to teach. Neither those without vision ("those who have studied and learned these precepts and still do not understand the obscurities of the Holy Scriptures")[69] nor those with only vision ("those who exult in divine assistance")[70] can make proper sense of the obscure passages, for one lacks the divine spark, the other, the necessary human link. Both are essential to understanding Scripture; the hermeneutics proposed in the *De doctrina christiana* encompasses and relies upon their coexistence.

The passage cited above that defines Christ as the road concludes: "When we arrive at Him we arrive also at the Father . . . binding [*vinciente*] and, as it were, cementing [*adglutinante*] ourselves in the Holy Spirit through whom we may remain in the highest good, which is also immutable" (p. 29). The qualitative difference between the journey and the arrival is brought out here in a subtext referred to by the words *vinciente* and *adglutinante*. Each carries a second meaning of binding a wound, and, appearing together as they do with the second essentially glossing the first, they call up an earlier passage in which reading and Christ are discussed in the context of healing wounds:[71]

> Et quem ad modum medici cum alligant vulnera non incomposite sed apte id faciunt, ut vinculi utilitatem quaedam pulchritudo etiam consequatur, sic medicina sapientiae per hominis susceptionem nostris est accommodata vulneribus, de quibusdam contrariis curans et de quibusdam similibus. . . . Quia ergo per superbiam homo lapsus est, humilitatem adhibuit ad sanandum. Serpentis sapientia decepti sumus, dei stultitia liberamur. . . . Ad eadem contraria pertinet quod etiam exemplo virtutum eius vitia nostra curantur. Iam vero similia quasi ligamenta membris et vulneribus nostris adhibita illa sunt, quod per feminam deceptos per feminam natus, homo homines . . . liberavit.

> And just as physicians when they bind up wounds do not do so haphazardly but neatly so that a certain beauty accompanies the utility of the bandages, so the medicine of Wisdom by taking on humanity is accommodated to our wounds, healing some by contraries and some by similar things. . . . Because man fell through pride, He applied humility as a cure. We were trapped by the wisdom of the serpent; we are freed by the foolishness of God. . . . The same principle of contraries is illustrated in the fact that the example of His virtues cures our vices. But the following things are like similar bandages applied to our wounds and members: that, born of a woman, He freed those deceived by a woman; that as a man He freed men. . . .[72]

In this passage Christ the healer is shown to be patching up the wounds of the past. He is clearly providing a good reading of an obscure or ambiguous passage: even as a wound is bound with a bandage of similar or opposite shape, so a good reader applies such a bandage to the obscure scriptural passage. Even as the sins of the Old Testament are righted by parallel events described in the New Testament, so a good reading will draw on parallel passages from each to right the reading of the other. Yet the true healing, like the full discovery and enjoyment of the truth, comes only from God. As human beings we can do no more than apply the suitable bandages—follow the charitable path—toward the truth that heals.

Of particular interest in this passage is the further insight it gives us into the hermeneutics of charity. What we are to gloss is here described not as a footprint but as a wound. Our job as readers is to locate the wounds in the text—the spots where the text is not of a piece—and through our reading bandage the text. Such a reading may well, it suggests, veil rather than reveal. By adding text to text—exegesis to Scripture—by building up rather than paring down, we establish a suitable context for obtaining the truth. Further, even as a bandage acknowledges the existence of a wound even as it simulates bonding, so our reading will make use of rifts to come to higher unities.

The image of a wounded text—of a rift that gives rise to commentary—brings us back momentarily to Cicero, who provides a means of understanding the fullest implications of this hermeneutics and thereby of proposing the way in which it informed subsequent texts. For Cicero, *inventio* is the process by which the orator locates the *constitutiones*, or points of disagreement, on which he will build his argument.[73] These *constitutiones* are thus comparable to Augustine's ambiguous or obscure passages: each allows for discussion; each requires interpretation; in each rhetoric the aim of "finding" is to locate these obscurities. What is different between the two—a difference implied, I would suggest, by Augustine's alteration of Cicero's noun *inventio* to the gerund *inveniendo*—is that while Cicero sees the argument of the speech as the establishment of a structure that encloses the right meaning and exiles the wrong,[74] Augustine sees reading as the motion from one to the other, a motion that recognizes both poles, acknowledges the existence of each, and asserts that the true reading, the

charitable reading, is that which will acknowledge the difference between the two, as well as the path from one to the
other. While the doctrine of *de inventione* asserts the necessity of
suppression and monumentalization, that of *de inveniendo*
emphasizes the power of becoming.

Augustine's reworking of this central rhetorical concept of
invention insists upon a new role for the interpreter, be it
speaker or audience, and new possibilities for the text. For
while humanist rhetoric insists on the suppression and subli-
mation of that which is not in keeping with its argument,
Augustine suggests that the point of an interpretation—be it
sermon or private reading—is to explore the area between the
literal cupidinous statement and the traced charitable one. We
are thus asked to participate in the text to the extent of
identifying a passage as ambiguous and then finding the
charitable other to cover this rift. Conversely, new texts
written for audiences trained in this manner would be inclined
to build in ambiguities of one form or another that would
employ such interpretative mechanics.

It is not hard to find sacred texts that demonstrate this
particular phenomenon. What is more interesting, however, is
that it is no more difficult to locate secular texts that show
evidence of this approach to persuasion. For this hermeneutics
of charity is not, I would suggest, inherently sacred. Nothing
about the procedure insists upon a sacred reading; the traced
level need not be charity. Rather, the goal need only be
something that is by definition unreachable within the limits
and strictures of language, the journey to which is motivated
by desire. For Augustine this something was God, yet it can
easily be translated into other forms of the ineffable. What is
truly new and ultimately most important about the *de inveniendo*, and the annunciatiory model, is that in suggesting a
new relationship between text and audience, it opens up new
possibilities for literature. Because it functions as does a
mathematical limit—always approaching but never attaining
the zero of the other—this hermeneutics can be applied to texts

of all sorts and, conversely, can free authors to express that which is usually suppressed. What Augustine develops in the *De doctrina christiana* is a new method that has a profound effect on the scope and nature of all interpretation, and all texts, that follow.

4 Rhetorical Anxiety in Troubadour Lyric

Augustinian Inheritance

Augustine reintroduces desire into rhetorical strategy. His language acknowledges a correspondence between his new rhetorical method and the ways of love or charity. As a result, however, he is forced to write himself out of the text and is left, as orator, in a precarious position. For while, on the one hand, Augustine advocates a rhetoric that offers more possibilities for pursuing varied truths than are offered by classical rhetoric, on the other, the way these new options become available is quite explicitly through a transfer of control from the orator to the audience. The structure of the new rhetoric, insisting as it does that desire be reinstated in a central position, insists as well that the text constantly work around a core, or toward a goal, that cannot be put into words. The orator can do little but guide, and while Augustine's rhetoric allows for dealing with truth and with states that cannot be articulated in language, it does not explain how the orator is to retain control over his text, his audience, and his meaning.

There are, in fact, two schools of thought on Augustine's rhetorical theories, the one seeing him as successful in his attempt to establish a new rhetoric, the other, not. The first takes him at his word and regards his rhetoric as a reworking of humanist concepts that allows for the exploration of such mysteries as Christ and the Christian life offer.[1] The second strain, very much in vogue now, suggests that Augustine's worldview as represented through his rhetorical system was not at all new, that it was as repressive as the humanist's and in many of the same ways. These critics show how Augustine, instead of freeing the darker forces, is still locked in a humanist system of thought, and, as evidence, they point to two different aspects of Augustine's writing: many of his works are carefully structured along Ciceronian lines,[2] and where fragmentation does occur it leads to silence, the void.

I would agree that Augustine's new rhetoric, when applied outside the sacred domain, was ultimately a failure. His attempted revamping of classical rhetoric, while revolutionary in theory, did not always hold up in practice. And yet Augustine's rhetorical assumptions, particularly as expressed in the *De doctrina christiana*, had tremendous impact on works of the Middle Ages, theoretical and practical alike. His ideas did mark a major shift in the rhetorical paradigm, and while that may have had less political or social impact than desired, the effect on rhetorical assumptions was significant indeed.

In order to make this argument, however, I will need to establish where real innovation did occur. Let me summarize briefly what changes were effected by Christian rhetoric.

- *Cupiditas* is redefined and granted a new function: goal not goad.
- Language is forced to defer to a higher authority.
- The orator is forced to defer to a higher authority; Annunciation, not Fall, becomes the model.
- Audience becomes the locus of truth and meaning.
- Rhetoric functions along the order of love, not of reason.

This list suggests that whatever positive factors the new

rhetoric will offer will come at the expense of the orator's control. That is, the more the new rhetoric is really developed and used, the less language and the orator will be in control of the outcome of the speech.

Such are the theoretical possibilities offered by Augustine's rhetoric, and such, as we have seen, are the ways it works out in some of the earliest Christian works, such as the catacomb paintings and the apologetic texts. It is up to the audience to provide the divine spark and, like Mary, to incarnate the text, to create from words a meaning that takes shape in a new and different medium and thus transcends purely linguistic bounds.

But every Christian orator has two personae: one that controls the audience and owes a lot to the humanists, the other that listens and translates while interpreting. Classical rhetorical practices do not disappear, for both rhetoric and literature draw at least some of their strength from presenting the world as we know it, as unified and understandable. The new position Christian rhetoric opens up, however, is that the other side of life—that which is ordered by love and desire—has a structure and a rhetoric all its own, a structure that is never immediately apparent nor always explicable. It is a structure that is different from but not necessarily inferior to the rational, and from a Christian perspective it deserves to be the bearer of truth.

In short, the hermeneutics of charity is not in the strict sense a hermeneutics at all. Rather, it is a defiance of hermeneutics, a nod toward a higher power who cannot be explained. In its negative capability, however, it enables us to understand the workings of medieval texts without reducing them to codes and systems. The hermeneutics of charity offers a system of nonrational understanding that demonstrates without explaining. Even as the rational must ultimately, on some level, give way to the divine spark, so the method of understanding tries to put mystery before, or at least alongside, reason.

The hermeneutics of charity—Augustine's new rhetoric—provides a key to one particular body of works: the lyrics of

the troubadours. Much has been made of the apparent connections between Augustine and the troubadours, and many
useful insights have been established from this application.
Augustine is indeed a useful way to approach most erotic
literature, as is Plato; Augustine is particularly valid for the
troubadours because they are explicitly concerned with issues
of desire and performance. What I wish to do in the following
chapter, however, is to suggest that the troubadours' use of
Augustine is comparable to Vergil's use of the humanist
orator. Patterning themselves on Augustinian orators, the
troubadours aim not to support the rhetorical doctrine but to
question it.

Private Power, Public Anxiety

The troubadours are the abandoned children of Western
literature, as they acknowledge little about their origin or
heritage. This fact has long led critics to assume that their
lyrics were sui generis. While Guilhem IX, the first known
troubadour, clearly refers to a preceding tradition of some
kind, that tradition seemed impossible to determine, imbed-
ded as it is in obscure references and novel techniques and
subjects. Recently, however, this assumption has been shown
to be fallacious. While the troubadour lyrics are certainly
different from the mainstream tradition of Latin lyrics, connections have been established between these two traditions.[3]
Troubadour lyric has been shown to employ much of the
Latin structure of thought—such as grammar and Ovidian
myth—and to employ it at will: Joan M. Ferrante has demonstrated that the troubadours' position outside the mainstream
was deliberately chosen and that they were perfectly able to
call upon a vast store of Latin techniques when it served their
purpose.[4]

As we have seen in the previous chapters, however, rhetoric
unmasks the unwilled. That is, although any author is free to
invent his plot and create his characters, he ultimately is not in
control—at least not entirely—of the assumptions that govern

his attitude toward, and relationship with, his audience. Such connections are part of an author's unconscious cultural baggage.

Moreover, it now seems fair to suggest that a literary text with an orator-protagonist is in all probability a literary text that confronts its culture's assumptions. As rhetoric appears to be linked, at least in the Western tradition, with value, the protagonist as orator can often easily depict the system—he is the system personified; his relationships reflect those of the culture of which he is part.

Within the framework of the troubadour tradition, but particularly in its early stages, one can find echoes of the Augustininan rhetorical tradition. While such an approach does not apply to all lyrics—the troubadours were responding to many different calls—it can account for the recurrence of certain themes and attitudes. Within the corpus of early troubadour lyric and, to a more limited extent, the later songs as well, there appears a concerted effort on the part of the poets to confront, present, question, and reject the bases of Augustinian rhetoric.

The word *troubadour* is derived from the Provençal *trobar* which has the same connotations as the Latin *invenire:* both have primary meanings of "to find" and secondary, technical meanings of isolating a rhetorical argument. This is not just an etymological game; many troubadours mention the fact of their performance,[5] suggest that their poetry is a form of oratory, and, most important, draw a connection between the performance and its subject: to love is to sing, to sing, to love. What they are singing about is precisely what they are doing, their songs are about their oratory.[6] Also, it is important to keep in mind that the lyrics were performed in front of a live audience, and, while we have little archaeological evidence of these performances, we can hypothesize that they involved rhetorical strategies, a supposition supported by the growing fascination of the troubadour with developing and identifying unique styles, such as *trobar leu* and *trobar clus.*[7]

The rhetorical expectations of the early troubadours—and presumably of their audience as well—are Augustinian. Superficially, the constants of troubadour song reflect a perception of persuasion that is consistent with the incarnational model proposed by Augustine. More important, however, the rhetorical assumptions of the troubadour as reflected in his lyrics and in his relationship with his audience appear to be Augustinian. The genre itself suggests this: by choosing a lyric form the troubadour is best able to fit into the contemplative role of *orans* established by Augustine. While Vergil's hero is public-spirited, Augustine's is focused on the individual. Vergil writes an epic, Augustine an epic in a lyric voice. The troubadour, in choosing lyric as genre and oration as focus, continues the Augustinian tradition. In choosing lyric that is specifically for public performance, however, he opens up the possibility for questioning Augustine, much as Vergil questions the assumptions of classical rhetoric. In externalizing and actualizing Augustinian tropes the troubadour comes to suggest where such a rhetoric is limited and to point outside its confines to a territory beyond. Such an anti-Augustinian movement has been demonstrated vis-à-vis the early troubadours and their attitudes toward time; I propose to extend this notion into their approaches to desire and power in rhetorical strategy.[8]

That Augustinian oratory had some influence on troubadour lyric has been suggested by many critics, most notably Frederick Goldin.[9] Yet the poems used as proof of this argument also speak, I believe, to the differences between the poiesis of the troubadours and Augustine's rhetoric. Jaufre Rudel's renowned *canso* "Lanqan li jorn" highlights through its specific use of Augustinian vocabulary precisely the problems the troubadour is facing.

The poem begins as follows:

> Lanqan li jorn son lonc en mai
> m'es bels doutz chans d'auzels de loing,
> e qan me sui partitz de lai
> remembra'm d'un'amor de loing:

vau de talan embroncs e clis
si que chans ni flors d'albespis
no·m platz plus que l'iverns gelatz.

When the days are long in May
I love the sweet song of distant birds,
And when I have left that place
I remember a distant love:
I am burdened and bowed down with desire,
So that neither song nor hawthorn flower
Pleases me more than icy winter.[10]

As Spitzer and others have pointed out, the language and imagery of this lyric suggest a worldview that is clearly comparable to Augustine's. The emphasis on desire, the necessary distance of the desired one from the one desiring in the basic "landscape" of the poem, and the explicit connection Jaufre establishes between his role of lover and that of a pilgrim[11] links this poem with the idea of desire and the pursuit of truth and satisfaction that Augustine discusses in the *De doctrina*.[12] But as we mentioned in the previous chapter, the thrust of this imagery in the *De doctrina* is that both the journey and the arrival provide satisfaction: instead of seeing the necessary distance from God and truth as frustrating, Augustine suggests that such a gap provides necessary room in which the divine spark can occur. While Jaufre establishes a context that is superficially comparable to the one Augustine describes, he suggests that his version is not fulfilling. For him, no crossing occurs in the space between lover and lady, no divine spark. Instead, this is a poem of frustration, a poem that uses the sacred model in a secular world.[13]

While Jaufre is the troubadour most known for the *amor de lonh*,[14] this theme appears in one of the earliest troubadour songs, Guilhem IX's "Farai chansoneta nueva," where he speaks of a love that has distanced him ("amors mi deslonja").[15] Although the attribution of this lyric has been questioned, a related Augustinian metaphor appears in Guilhem's "Mout jauzens me prenc en amar," where he uses the image of a journey (line 4: "anar"; the significance is reinforced by its being the first word to rhyme with *amar*) together with the idea of a lady beyond description, who can turn all things to their opposites:

> Per son joy pot malautz sanar
> E per sa ira sas morir
> E savis hom enfolezir
> E belhs hom sa beutat mudar
> E·l plus cortes vilaneiar
> E·l totz vilas encortezir.

> Through her joy a sick man can become well,
> And through her anger a healthy man can die
> And a wise man become foolish
> And a handsome man lose his beauty
> And the most refined become boorish
> And the most boorish become refined.[16]

I would suggest that the troubadour retains three essential factors of Augustinian oratory: an emphasis on desire as organizing force, an inscribed female audience, and the internal conflict facing the Augustinian orator vis-à-vis control of his audience and his meaning. In each instance, however, this structure of oratory proves a cause of anxiety, and the troubadour, by taking a deliberate stance on the rhetorical assumptions of his time, acknowledges that such a rhetoric of desire is ultimately ineffectual in a secular world even as it is absolutely essential to the structure of the poet's imagination.

For while troubadour lyric asserts an equivalence between desire of man for God and desire of man for woman, the end result is not the same. In order to demonstrate fully the differences between these two systems it is necessary to return briefly to Augustine and examine his sexual assumptions. In asserting an incarnational model for persuasion, and in drawing on the passage from the Seventh Letter as process, Augustine, as we suggested in the last chapter, sees persuasion as occurring in the crossing between two opposites: between the verbal and the visual, between the word and metaphor. Yet

that crossing is a troping, and a trope that must remain to some
degree potential: it is the trope that causes creation. If that
trope is ever reified it cannot work, and if its requisite elements
are ever literalized it will not function. It must remain metaphoric and potential and must consist of desire motivated by
will and participation. This is clear in Augustine, both in his
use of the Seventh Letter, whose description of the divine spark
is phrased as a simile ("like a flame kindled by a leaping
spark"), and his insistence in the last books of the *Confessions*
that man can participate in the divine creation if he willfully
gives up control of that creation. But what is equally clear in
Augustine, and not in the Seventh Letter, is that this process
involves some threatening sexual assumptions as well. If we
are to create and persuade in this way, we must become like
Mary: our turning is a sexual turning that transforms us, for
the time of creation, into the willing ancilla of God. Our
acceptance of that role gives us a chance of experiencing the
divine truth. While on a metaphoric level this transfer may be
acceptable and possible, on the applied level it is neither. For
what is really implied in this process is the erasure of sexual
difference: man assumes a woman's role in the creative process
in order to experience the divine.

Troubadour lyric speaks to this disjuncture. A well-known
fact about troubadour poetry is that its inscribed audience was
predominantly female. Whatever the historical cause or reality
of this may have been, the fact that it was not only mentioned
by the troubadour but used to organize his thought and
performance suggests that it played a significant part in his
poetics. Because the troubadours frequently allude to the
"female" quality of their audience, together with their use of
performance as a way of commenting on their poiesis, it is
likely that the female addressee provided a significant aspect
of their self-perception: it was, in other words, important for
reasons other than just the given song or given performance
that the audience assume a female persona.

Such an allegorized and abstracted role for woman is not

unique to the troubadours; it has roots in precisely the rhetorical tradition we have been pursuing. In the late tenth or early eleventh century, Notker III,—or Notker Labeo, as he was known —wrote a treatise entitled *De arte rhetorica* in which he proposed to outline a "new rhetoric," new in respect to the old rhetoric of Aristotle and Cicero, as Samuel Jaffe has so persuasively demonstrated.[17] The text lays out the five parts of rhetoric, as in Cicero, and ends, as one would expect, with a section entitled "De pronuntiatione.[18] This section begins with a definition of *pronuntiatio* and proceeds through a discussion of what constitutes an appropriate presentation. Notker covers issues like the amount of food one should eat before speaking, the loudness of the voice, and so on, and ends by advising that a speaker's gestures should not be too soft, nor his lateral movements too womanly, nor his neck arched. Such allurements, though charming, he says, are nonetheless not considered manly and hence are not suitable for the orator, even as dramatic histrionics are equally inappropriate.[19]

That Notker finds it important to emphasize the undesireability of feminine qualities and, one can deduce, of seduction is crucial, and points to a larger connection between him and the greater rhetorical tradition of which he and the troubadours were a part. For his uneasiness with desire suggests a connection between him and the humanist tradition; in an important way, Notker's treatise is reminiscent of Cicero's. Both insist on the exclusion of desire in order to ensure the proper functioning of the system. But, as Notker tells us in a letter to Bishop Hugo von Sitten, his purpose is not just to return to a classical rhetoric; rather, he intends to offer something new, and the language of his treatise suggests where this newness lies: his rejection of the feminine at the end of his text has been balanced by a call for her return, in different form, at its start. The treatise begins as follows:

> Olim disparuit cuius facies depingenda est et quae nostram excedit memoriam. eam qualis formare difficile est, quia

multi dies sunt ex quo desivit esse. Oporteret eam inmor-
talem esse, cuius amore languent, ita homines ut abstractam
tam diu et mundo mortuam resurgere velint. ubi cato ubi
cicero domestici eius? Nam si illi redirent ab inferis haec illis
ad usum sermonis famularetur sine qua nihil eis certum
constabat quod ventilandum esset pro rostris. Quid autem
est quod in suam non redigatur originem? Naturalis eloquentia viguit quousque ei per doctrinam filia successit
artificialis quae deinde rhetorica dicta est. Haec postquam
antiquitate temporis extincta est, illa iterum revixit. Unde
hodieque plurimos cernimus qui in causis solo naturali
instinctu ita sermone callent ut quae velint quibuslibet facile
suadeant nec tamen regulam doctrinae ullam requirant.

Long ago she disappeared, whose appearance I am to depict
and who has passed beyond the scope of our memory. It is
difficult to describe her as she was, for much time has passed
since she went away. It was presumed that she was immor-
tal by those who loved her, and so men wish that she,
taken away as if dead, be returned to earth, having been
away so long. Where are her servants, Cato and Cicero? For
if they came back from the underworld she would be put
in the service of speech-making; without her nothing was
composed by those which was aired at the rostrum. What is
there that does not return to its origins? Natural eloquence
flourished until her artificial daughter, called rhetoric, suc-
ceeded her through teaching. Rhetoric passed away after
antiquity, and eloquence was again revived. And so today we
see many who become skilled in debate by instinct alone and
who wish to easily persuade whatever they wish, not using
the rule of any teaching.[20]

"She," in this case, is not desire but rhetoric itself, and her
long absence is lamented. Juxtaposing this opening passage
with the passage at the end produces the following insights.
Two women are present in this text: one the much-desired
rhetoric, who has long been away, the other all-too-present
desire, who must be exiled if rhetoric is to proceed effectively.
The allegorical woman and the real feminine: a dual vision of
the female, but also, I would suggest, a dual and conflicting

vision of the rhetorical tradition. For even as the exile of desire with which the text ends has precedent in the humanist tradition, so the lament over the long-awaited return of the desired one has precedent in the rhetorical tradition of Augustine.

Notker is not just talking about the return of rhetoric here. He is also setting up a situation in which desire for the absent female is valorized. While this would appear to be in direct contradiction with rhetoric as the humanists define it, it corresponds well to the Christian rhetorical tradition as articulated by Augustine. As we have seen, the major innovation Augustinian rhetoric offers is the valorization of desire, or will, as motivating force of persuasion. In order to communicate the truth, Augustine asserts, will must be present in both speaker and audience. Truth must ultimately flash upon the soul like, as the Seventh Letter says, a flame kindled by a leaping spark. Augustine's rhetorical works consequently propose a balance between the rational and the irrational, and between reason and faith.

Above all, then, Augustinian rhetoric implies a dialogue of powers in which reason is balanced by faith and will, speaker by audience, male by female. For the orator, however, such a model is ultimately restrictive, as the absolute authority of the orator over his audience is denied. Instead of being in control of his medium or his audience, the Augustinian orator plays only one part in a dialogue. Truth resides outside of his domain; he is bound to an indeterminate dialogue whose power lies outside of his control and with God.

While this shift in control may not be threatening to an Augustinian preacher, it presents certain difficulties when applied in a nontheological context, such as the secular court. Even as Notker projects a dual view of the role of women and desire in the rhetorical situation, so the troubadours establish two very different roles for women to fill. In the Guilhem IX lyric "Mout jauzens me prenc en amar," quoted above, the woman is desired for her curative powers but feared for the possible negative effect she may have on the poet-lover.

Not only do the early troubadours give women and desire a dual treatment, they also take as one of their central issues the problem of control, and on this subject they are equally confusing. Guilhem IX's "Farai un vers de dreit nïen" will serve as example:

> I'll do a song about nothing at all,
> It won't be about me nor about others,
> It won't be about love nor about happiness,
> Nor about anything else. . .
> I don't know what time I was born,
> I am not happy or sad,
> I am not a stranger or an intimate friend,
> Nor can I do anything about it.[21]

Criticism of this poem falls into two main camps.[22] On the one side we have those best represented by E. Köhler, who argues that the poem is an example of negative theology—*nescio quid*—a poem, in other words, that explores the ineffable by negating the rational and known.[23] Lynne Lawner, the most sensible critic for the opposing side, sees the poem as largely ironic. It is not about not-knowing, Lawner says, but rather about a special kind of knowing—a feigned not-knowing. There is "never the possibility that the poet does not know what the poem, or, for that matter, the world, is about."[24]

While I would certainly agree that this lyric is not a serious probe into the metaphysical, I do not follow Lawner in the assertion that the poet is entirely in control of his world. Rather, I think there are indications of a troublesome issue that stems from troubadour self-definition. While the first line is usually translated much as Gerald Bond has, with *de dreit nïen* rendered as "about nothing," "from nothing" is also a possible reading: the medieval English preacher Peter Pateshull uses the phrase *de nihil* in place of *ex nihilo* in a parody sermon; the substitution, while not common, does occur. As such, *de dreit nïen* could be seen as a translation of precisely the Latin phrase with which contemporary philosophers were so concerned: *ex nihilo*.[25]

While a full-length discussion of twelfth-century cosmological theories is beyond the scope of this investigation, it will be useful to mention a few facts relating to the central group of philosophers, the so-called School of Chartres, who were as important to the their intellectual climate as Aristotle was to Cicero's and Vergil's. While these men differed in the details of their solutions to problems posed, they all, at one time or another, confronted the issue of creation, both cosmological and cosmogenic. Their discussion focuses on a debate inherited from Augustine and Boethius over whether God created *ex nihilo* and over the nature of any secondary creation.[26] That this is a significant issue to this eminent group of thinkers at this time is of central concern to us; the particular solutions they offer are not as crucial. For their interest in creation suggests that the issues we have been looking at—the relation of man's rhetoric to God's, and of man's control to God's— were again important.

Let me quote, in part, what one of the Chartrians— Guillaume of Conches—wrote about creation and the cosmos: "While they say that all is made from the four elements and not from nothing, and that the four elements exist according to two principles, atoms and void, the space in which the atoms move, we say that all inferior bodies that are both generated and corruptible are indeed made from these four elements, but the elements themselves were created *ex nihilo* by God."[27]

There is a clear distinction here, echoed by other Chartrians and by Abelard, between the creation by God, which was performed *ex nihilo*, and man's creations, which consist of a rearrangement of pre-existing matter. There is also a clear delineation between the creators involved, for man, it is implied, does not and cannot create as God does. While these philosophers never specifically discuss oration, the definition of the orator would be affected by just such questioning. Instead of offering a resolution to the problem of authority in language suggested in the Augustinian model, Guillaume of Conches and other Chartrians emphasize the great difference between man's orations and God's, as they suggest even more clearly that the power of real illumination and insight is removed entirely from the hands of the orator: he can re-create, (often through such activities as exegesis) and through his re-creations he can understand his Creator and his ways. But this re-creation is of a different kind from his Creator's: while he may uncover an order of love, he must argue by relying on logic and the rational powers of language.

Guilhem IX's assertion that he can create in his medium just as God does in his suggests that other assumptions have changed as well. Stanzas 4 and 6 of this poem bear out this contention: stanza 4 takes as its topic the right kind of doctor ("Metge querrai al mieu albir"), while stanza 6 speaks of the right kind of woman ("Qu'ie·n sai gensor e belazor, / E que mais vau"). These two strophes contrast two kinds of knowing: the kind that affects us here and now, and the kind of abstract and removed truth that must be taken on faith. Guilhem is making an argument for the more immediate as being the more useful. The real lady who can be seen, the doctor who makes actual physical pain go away—these, he says, are worth the most to him.[28]

These strophes support my reading of the opening lines. In stating that he will create, like God, *de dreit nïen*, Guilhem IX is suggesting a recasting of an entire worldview to one in which the poet has authority, in which he, like God, is in control of his universe. By saying that the abstract neo-Platonic doctors and women aren't worth an ant or a rooster (lines 17, 34), Guilhem suggests that that which he controls is worth more. Relative concepts—of knowing, of seeing, of being—are here questioned, and old values rejected in favor of new.

By offering a comparison between poet and God, Guilhem also anticipates a rejection of Augustine's rhetoric. The balance proposed in Augustine's rhetorical works between the rational and the irrational, and between speaker and audience, is restrictive because the absolute authority of the orator over an audience and through language is denied. Instead of being in control of his medium or his audience, the Augustinian orator participates in only one part of a conversation. He is bound to an indeterminate dialogue whose power lies beyond his control—with God and his audience. Guilhem, in his assertion that he can create *de dreit nïen* and in his valuing of the seen over the unseen, is, I would suggest, proposing a new hierarchical relationship between speaker and audience that would offer the orator, once again, the reins of control.

The pseudo-epistemological poem of Raimbaut d'Aurenga titled "Escotatz, mas no say que s'es" elaborates on this stance as it develops both the creation imagery and the imagery of relative value.[29] It takes Guilhem IX's ideas further, however, as it suggests several inherent problems with such a reordering. Essentially a poem about the value of the immediate, "Escotatz" also illustrates that every troubadour poet is also a lover and, as a lover, is not capable of asserting a different, non-Augustinian set of assumptions.[30]

Like Guilhem IX, Raimbaut d'Aurenga takes on an academic genre: textual exegesis. His poem is organized in prosimetrum, with the prose commenting, as Dante will later in the *Vita nuova*, on his own lyrics. Within the exegetical format, he creates his own quasi-spiritual text, a fact he reiterates through his "baptizing" it at the end: "Er finisc mo no-say-que-s'es / C'aisi l'ay volgut batejar" ('Now I finish my no-say-que-s'es / For so I wish to baptize it"). He elucidates his scripture through his exegesis and so takes on two roles, that of God the creator and that of man the commentator in his role as reader. But as creator he, like Guilhem IX, is playful and nonsensical, and so suggests a questioning of rhetorical assumption.

In the first strophe of this *canso* Raimbaut d'Aurenga outlines what is expected of him as poet: he doesn't know what he is creating, but he knows that if he doesn't finish it the audience will not consider it a composition: "Ni ges no say co·l mi fezes / S'aytal no·l podi acabar" ("I do not know how I should construct it if I weren't able to finish it"); and again, in the second strophe: "Car si ieu vos o avia mogut, e no·us o trazia a cap, tenriatz m'en per fol" ("If I had begun it for you, and didn't bring it to a conclusion, you would consider me a fool"). This, then, is what the audience expects: a finished poem—more than a recognizable form. Interlaced with this argument is a related one similar to that of Guilhem IX: Raimbaut d'Aurenga refers to relative value, and, like Guilhem, says that what he has is worth more than what he does not have: "Car mais amaria seis deniers en mon punh que mil sols el cel" ("For I should prefer six sous in my hand to a thousand "suns" in the sky") and "Tot cant es non pres un pojes / Vas so c'ades vey et esgar" ("I do not value all that exists a farthing compared to that which I now see and behold"). Finished, completed objects are what the audience expects from the speaker and what the speaker likewise considers of value.

Unlike Guilhem IX, however, Raimbaut d'Aurenga places this set of values in a larger context. For while Guilhem speaks only of the control of the poet, Raimbaut d'Aurenga suggests that such control, at least at his time, has as its counterpoint a situation in which he has no control—namely, as lover. As W. T. H. Jackson has pointed out,[31] the troubadour always plays two roles, that of poet and that of lover. As a poet, he may well assert control, as both Guilhem and Raimbaut do; as lover, however, he is not free to do so. This is best illustrated by the issue of completion. While the audience expects the poet to finish his work, the lady, by contrast, is not expected to finish hers: "Tot ayso dic per una domna que·m fay languir ab belas paraulas et ab lonc respieg, no say per que" ("All this I say because of a lady who makes me languish with fine promises and long expectation, I don't know why"). Raimbaut makes the comparison even clearer when in poem 13 he uses the verb *acabar* to refer to the fulfillment of a relationship: "Si sa grans merces m'acaba / Mon car desir qu'ai tan volgut" ("if her great favor brings to conclusion my dear desire which I have yearned for so much"). The verb in this case is identical to the one used of his poetic composition in the knowing poem: *acabar* ("bring to a head"). While the audience expects him to *acabar* his poem, the lady, traditionally, refuses to *acabar* their relationship. Two sets of relationships are paralleled and contrasted here: on the one hand, that of the poet and his audience, on the other, that of the lover and the lady. Not only does the poet assert control over his audience and show an ability to fulfill their expectations by completing his work ("si hom li demanda qui l'a fag, pot dir que sel que sap be far totas fazendas can se vol"; "if they ask him who made it, he can say one who knows how to do all deeds well when he wants to"), but the lover reflects a similar wish, which traditionally is not fulfilled. As speaker he completes his work, as lover he has no control.

This double standard reflects a clash of rhetorical expectations, and the troubadours' inability to reconcile their two personae articulates a rhetorical crisis. As poet, the troubadour, be he Guilhem IX or Raimbaut d'Aurenga, is in control—of language, of medium, of audience. He can and does create *ex nihilo* and so controls the truth of his poem. As lover, however, he articulates the position of an Augustinian orator who must wait for his audience to complete the dialogue.

Both Guilhem IX and Raimbaut d'Aurenga repudiate the Augustinian model, Guilhem celebrating the power of the poet outside of Augustine's worldview, Raimbaut pointing out through the dual persona of every troubadour the desirability—and difficulty—of rejecting such a system. Both suggest that such a shift is for the good; both assert a real desire to act on their world as they wish. Both also suggest, however, that such a revolution in thought may for a while have to be confined to the poetic realm—that while as poets they can indeed control and finish what they set out to do, as lovers they cannot yet assert such a force in their worlds. The voice of the lover—frustrated, impatient—is, I would suggest, the voice of the Augustinian orator in a secular context.

It is for this reason as well, I believe, that most of the early troubadours start their poems with a word that emphasizes the distinction between their role in the work, and their role in the

world: Guilhem ix uses *farai* ("I will make"); other troubadours use comparable words that emphasize their ability to
create, *ex nihilo*, through poetry. So too the troubadours
emphasize their power over standard topoi, most notably the
Natureingang. The troubadours use these standard opening
tropes not to attach themselves to the Latin tropic tradition that
Curtius has made so famous but to mark their departure from
that tradition. So Raimbaut d'Aurenga sings:

> Ar resplan la flors enversa
> Pels trencans rancx e pels tertres,
> Cals flors? Neus, gels e conglapis
> Que cotz e destrenh e trenca;
> Don vey morz quils, critz, brays, siscles
> En fuelhs, en rams e en giscles
> Mas mi ten vert e jauzen Joys
> Er quan vey secx los dolens croys.

Now the "reversed flower" shines among the sharp cliffs
and among the hills. What flower? Snow, ice, and frost
which stings and hurts and cuts; wherefore I see calls, cries,
songs and warblings dead among the leaves, the branches,
and the twigs. But Joy keeps me green and gay now when
I see the grievous evil persons withered.[32]

The disjuncture here noted between the world outside and
the world within points again to the issue of control. For while
Raimbaut seems to suggest that he is in control—that within
the bounds of his poems and imagination he can create as he
will—the use of the *Natureingang* topos emphasizes the limits
of that control and the truth of the Chartrian adaptation of
Augustinian thought: while the poet may have control, the
lover does not. While through poetry the poet can stop time
("A mos ops la˙m vuelh retenir: / Per lo cor dedins refrescar /
E per la carn renovellar/ Que no puesca envellezir"; "I want to
retain her for my own benefit / To refresh my heart within /
and to renew my flesh, /So that it cannot age") he can control
neither his love nor his lady.[33] In such examples, the

poetic persona assumes two separate voices, one for the poet, the other the lover.[34] While the poet strives to please the audience, the lover wishes to express his emotions about a particular lady. This division—apparent, for example, in many of Bernart de Ventadorn's *cansos*—can also be explained in a slightly different manner. Because the poet aims to please his audience, which is present as he performs, he strives to turn the poem into a celebration of the power of poetry to control and create. The lover, on the other hand, wishing to win favor from his lady, desires anything but the extension of the present. On the contrary, he wishes that his present lonely state be diminished in as great a degree as possible, and so points out his inability to do anything at all.

While the poet can control the world of his work, then, the lover cannot. The poet, therefore, can in fact create *ex nihilo*, as Guilhem IX and Raimbaut point out; the lover, however, must play the role of audience to his new "God," the lady, and suffer the whims of her wishes. While the poet, the lady, and love itself have the godlike power to create at will, the lover must suffer passively the consequences of their actions. If love does choose to help, its effect can be similar to that of the divine spark: "Chantars no pot gaire valer / si d'ins dal cor no mou lo chans, / ni chans no pot dal cor mover / si no i es fin'amors coraus" ("There is no use in singing if the song does not spring from the heart; and the song cannot spring from the heart if there is no true love there").[35] Without love, Bernart's persona is not an effective singer, even as words alone cannot bring about change in a Christian context.

In bringing Augustine's rhetoric out of a sacred context and suggesting that it bears the same relation to societal hierarchies as Cicero's did to his, the troubadours find that it does not work: desire for God is not desire for a lady, or at least is not resolved in a similar way; creation *ex nihilo* is not creation *de dreit nïen,* and, most particularly, *domna* is not *dominus.* For while Mary, in her divinity, listens and accepts, mortal woman, limited by her mortality, often only listens. In other words, the

lady of troubadour lyric is a Mary *manqué*: given the freedom
and power that Augustine's model implies, she nonetheless
lacks the charity of Mary and so abuses her privilege. Such a
clash of sacred and secular ideologies and expectations can be
seen in the fourth strophe of Raimbaut d'Aurenga's lyric
"Escotatz," in which he juxtaposes Latin and Provençal, slang
and biblical styles, as well as two different concepts of the lady:
"Dieus aiuda! In nomine patris et filii et spiritus sancti! Aiso,
que sera, domna?" In the context of the Trinity we think of
Mary; in his asking, "what'll it be, lady?" we find her deposed.
The troubadour lady does not have the powers of forgiveness
associated with the Trinity, and she is often represented as a
driving force, not one willed in any way by the poet–lover.
Perhaps most telling of all, her name suggests what she has
come to represent: *domna* bears the same relation to *dominus* in
the Christian structure that *patria* does to *pater* in the Vergilian
one: the *domna* of troubadour lyric is the *patria* in the *Aeneid*;
she is the masculine force masquerading as female, the force
that subsumes all time and energy yet is often not pursued by
will or personal desire.

So, for instance, in this later *canso* by Giraut de Borneil:

> Domna, aissi com us anheus
> Non a forsa contr'ad un ors,
> Sui eu, si la vostra valors
> No·m val plus frevols c'us rauzeus,
> Et er plus breus
> Ma vida que de cartel chartz
> S'oimais me pren negus destartz
> Que no·m fassatz drech de l'envers.
> Et tu, fin'amors, que me sofers,
> Que deus garar
> Los fis amans de foleiar,
> Sias me chabdeus e guirens
> A ma domna, pos aissi·m vens!

Lady, as a lamb is powerless against a bear, so am I,
wanting your strength, weaker than a reed. And my life will

be briefer than the fourth part of an instant now if any harm should come my way and you still deny me justice for all this neglect. And you, True Love, bear me up, preserve true lovers from doing foolish things, be my guide and witness with my lady, see now how she conquers me.[36]

Here the lover asks love for help in fending off the lady's effect on him. It seems, then, that although the lady in troubadour song assumes much of the power of God in the Augustinian schema and rhetoric, she often uses that responsibility and strength in anything but a charitable way while, at the same time, undermining the authority of the poet–lover. Rather than a hermeneutics of charity willed by the orator-audience, we find the schema reworked to suggest that the desired goal and object are no longer charitable. While the dynamics are the same for both Augustine and the troubadours, the shift into a secular context seems to bring with it a shift of motivation and hence of efficacy.

The examples provided so far are all drawn from *cansos*. Yet the reliance upon, and rejection of, the Augustinian model occurs in other subgenres as well. Perhaps the most telling example of how the Augustinian model is assumed and denied is another subgenre: the *alba*.[37] Though adapted from the Christian dawn hymn, the *alba*, or dawn song, presents the dawn instead as an unwanted event: an *alba* is a song of lovers who fear the inevitable separation that the dawn threatens to bring. On the surface, the *alba* is always riddled with anxiety, disturbed by the prospect of the impending dawn. But as a poem it is wonderfully ambivalent, as the dawn never does arrive in any Provençal *alba*, and so the alba is able to express clearly the ambivalence felt by the troubadour poet over his power and control.

In the *alba*, the negative force that the lady seems most often to incorporate is compared to the forces of nature and the sun. Yet it is possible, as I have shown elsewhere, that the rising sun, the *alba*, is to be associated with the Last Judgment and Christ's arrival as an avenging figure.[38] Hence the *alba* serves as an ideal example of how the forces and powers of the oratorical situation had changed: not only does the lady assume this role of Christ in the hermeneutics of charity, but this perception of the lady then seems to have a negative effect on the current perception of the Godhead. In the *alba*, she has become the force that opposes the forgiving all-seeing Father, associated rather with the avenging Christ of the Last Judgment.[39]

Even Christ is not allowed in the *alba* to be the charitable, all-forgiving God. Rather, he is the all-seeing, all-judging God of the Last Judgment. While the rhetorical model appears still to be that of Augustine—motivated by desire, not reason, and insisting on the participation of the speaker and audience—it suggests that the motivation is a desire to avoid rather than to achieve—fear and anxiety not satisfaction and love, riddle these songs.

The *alba* is also a perfect example of the ambivalent, double role assumed by the troubadour, for as poet he can indeed put off the dawn, and hence the moment of creation and illumination as well as of judgment. While on one level the narrative speaks of an anxiety-ridden anticipation of coming change, on another level that change is forestalled by the lyric itself. The dawn, however frightening on a referential level, remains a thing of the future within the confines of the poem.

Moreover, the narrator of the *alba* clearly speaks to the rhetorical problematics of the troubadour. In the Provençal *alba*—unlike the Christian dawn hymn, Middle High German *Tagenliede*, or Old French *aube*, the watchman assumes a central role.[40] He is the only speaking persona in many of the *alba*s and is a crucial figure in every one. He is the oral counterpart to the visual rising sun and the aural songs of the birds. It is through his interpretation of the natural signs that the dawn is reported or, in fact, created, as the dawn is here only a linguistic phenomenon, a space man creates whose actual existence cannot be determined. The watchman, as personification of this element, serves a double function, and his role parallels that of the troubadour poet: like the poet, the watchman both causes the rising of the sun and forestalls it.

This tension between having and lacking control can be seen not only in particular poems or certain genres, as above, but also in the taxonomy of the entire troubadour genre.[41] The *canso* was the most popular of all the Provençal subgenres because it speaks most directly to the issue of desire. In the other subgenres, however, the object changes even as the underlying tension remains motivated by the same issues. All troubadour lyrics express a desire for something unattained within the temporal and modal scope of the lyric itself; each distinguishes its brand of desire on the basis of how the "other," and change that leads to the "other," are to be defined. While the *canso* sings of desire for the lady, the *alba* sings for time to stand still, for the dawn not to arrive and the lover not to leave; in the *sirventes* the "other" is a better time in the past or future, while the *planh* yearns for a time that has passed. Desire, not reason, organizes the plots of these songs and provides their generating matrix; the needs of desire are what is being voiced here—in a way that would have made Juno proud and that echoes Augustine to a great degree.

Against this plot, though, runs the countertheme of the poet's control and power over his subject matter and audience. The impotence of the orator implicit in Augustinian rhetorical theory is specifically answered in the taxonomy of the troubadour lyric by the fact that, as static as the plot of the lyric is, the song always progresses from beginning to end. The beginnings of all troubadour lyrics are heavily marked, as are their endings, and the sense of the poet as one who can *acabar* a lyric, to use Raimbaut's phrase, is strong. In addition, these lyrics show the resurgence of a moral vocabulary associated with performance. Bernart de Ventadorn says that it is no miracle that he sings better than anyone else ("Non es meravelha s'eu chan / melhs de nul altre chantador"): he sings better because he loves better; he who does not love cannot sing. His love makes him a better person, and this moral improvement is what makes him a superior poet-orator.

I would suggest that troubadour song was, at least at the start, a movement intended to confront the methods of rhetoric available to the poet-orator and to show how ultimately limiting the Augustinian approach was. While the Augustinian structure is from time to time useful and productive within the confines of the imagination, as a rhetoric it is a failure, for while it establishes from the start a series of expectations for speaker and audience that in many ways reflect the sacred rhetoric discussed above, the end result is not the sublime but the void or the ridiculous. Like Christian rhetoric, troubadour lyric builds ambiguities in order to have them play off against each other in the minds of the audience; it leads, ultimately, to a higher inexpressible truth. Even the kind of ambiguities developed is the same: a situation of opposition is established, and the exegetical discipline required consists of traveling the path between, though never fully unifying, the two.

Yet the major difference between the two remains that while Augustinian rhetoric implies that such a process is a transcendent one, troubadour lyric constantly suggests that such a movement between produces only frustration or anxiety. Perhaps this comes from the fact that not all ambiguity leads to transcendent understanding. Without such an epiphany ambiguity can be little more than frustrating. As such, however, it faithfully represents the human condition, which, while only occasionally illuminated by a divine spark, is constantly thwarted by frustration.

Conclusion: Legacy
of the Divine Spark

Rhetoric, if understood as the relationship of reason to desire in persuasion, outlines a culture's unspoken assumptions; literature that foregrounds rhetoric often aims to confront and question those assumptions. Although different in many ways, the texts studied here—Vergil's *Aeneid*, Augustine's *Confessions* and *De doctrina christiana*, and the lyrics of the early troubadours—all have protagonists who are also orators,—true spokesmen for their cultures. What each protagonist upholds, however, each author holds up to question: the values attributed to Aeneas are not, it would appear, Vergil's own; Augustine the infant sign maker is not Augustine the preacher; the troubadour-lover is not the troubadour poet. Each text speaks to two rhetorical systems: the one presented clearly through the language and actions of the protagonist, the other hinted at indirectly in the reflexes of the author.

One can abstract the issues, as I have done to a certain extent here, in an attempt to clarify the motivation of each author for using a rhetorical model. The problem of the *Aeneid* becomes then a question of the place of will, desire, and mediation in the Roman world, in which reason is deemed more appropriate than desire. Augustine takes up this issue but proposes a new rhetoric that offers a balance between reason and desire, speaker and audience. Desire has been reincorporated into the rhetorical act. In order to attain truth—in order to be converted or even persuaded—one must employ both reason and desire, the latter valorized as will. Likewise, every act of oratory involves the willing participation of the audience.

The troubadours find themselves struggling within an intellectual framework they find restrictive. Ironically, the system Vergil had proposed and early Christianity developed proved ultimately unrealistic. For while classical rhetoric reflected a well-established and comprehensive worldview, Christian rhetoric did not. Rather, such reform as this rhetorical change brought about was limited to areas such as theology and philosophy. When applied in a secular context, a structure based on balance and mediation and motivated by will proved largely untenable, and the troubadours struggled to free themselves from it. For the reincorporation of desire into the rhetorical system had forced the orator to give up much of his control. While such a release may be liberating in a sacred context, it is inhibiting in a secular one, and a rhetoric that valorizes elements beyond the control of the rhetor is, ultimately, doomed to failure.

Perhaps the clearest evidence we have of the shift that occurs between one work and the next is the change in genre. While Vergil chooses epic, Augustine writes of an inner journey, and the troubadours write lyrics: the struggle between author and hero becomes increasingly internalized. This shift in genre can be seen as a direct result of the change in rhetorical expectation and emphasis. Epic necessitates a clear delineation between author and audience—performative and descriptive, it is also a genre that relies upon clear distinctions between author and work, and between speaker and audience. The inner epic of Augustine's *Confessions* suggests a breakdown of categories and distinctions, including author and work, and speaker and audience; Augustine's emphasis on the orator as part of his own audience is reflected in the identification he establishes between himself and his work and the one he invites between himself and his audience. The lyric of the troubadours, with its emphasis on the "I" and the explicit identification between the author and his work, is Augustine's inner journey made public. But the troubadour voice is not at one with itself or with its work. Emphatically a performed literature, troubadour lyric sings of the frustration of an orator who is not in control of his audience. As hybrid a genre as Augustine's lyric epic, troubadour song is, to a certain extent, a lyric that would be epic, as its author attempts to assert control over both audience and work. And from the troubadours it is but one small step to Dante, who will, in his *Divine Comedy*, write the epic lyric, and so foreground the shadowed rhetoric of the troubadours.

NOTES

Chapter 1. Vergil's Orator

1. Text is from the 1976 Oxford edition, ed. R. A. B. Mynors; translations are my own unless otherwise noted.
2. For a clear outline of this polarization, see Eugene Vance, "Warfare and the Structure of Thought in Vergil's *Aeneid*," *Quaderni Urbinati* 15(1973)111-62.
3. Isocrates, *Antidosis* 274-85, trans. G. Norlin, Loeb Edition (Cambridge, Mass.: Harvard University Press, 1929; rpt. 1962), vol. 2.
4. Isocrates, *Antidosis* 253-54.
5. George A. Kennedy, *Classical Rhetoric and Its Christian and Secular Tradition from Ancient to Modern Times* (Chapel Hill: University of North Carolina Press, 1980), p. 33.
6. This is shown as well by the overall structure of a speech as Cicero defines it. As civilization progresses from chaos to order, so speech begins in initial disagreement, a *constitutio*, and develops through the *exordium, narratio, partitio, confirmatio, reprehensio,* and *digressio* to the final agreement, or *conclusio,* called by some *peroratio*. Each successive part of a speech both acknowledges the initial disagreement and moves one step closer to bridging the gap that the disagreement has created.
7. L. A. Springer, "Vergil's Voice of Protest," *CW* 47(1953)55-57, suggests: "The figure of Cicero . . . may have been before Vergil when he composed one of his first similes—an appeal to reason in times of stress: 1.148-53."
8. It should be noted here that Cicero's own views on rhetoric change drastically through the course of his career and that the description offered in the *De inventione* is not one he would uphold later. See W. R. Johnson, *Luxuriance and Economy: Cicero and the Alien Style*

(Berkeley: University of California Press, 1971). However, as this early version does seem to coincide with the structure of the universe as Vergil first presents it, it would seem to warrant at least a brief look.

9. On technical aspects of Cicero's rhetoric, see L. Laurand, "L'art oratoire de Cicéron, théorie et practice," *Etudes Classiques* 1(1932)381-87; see also his bibliographic notes on Cicero in *Revue des Etudes Latines* 7(1929)348-69; R. Barilli, "La retorica di Cicerone," *Verri* 19(1966) 203-32. M. L. Clarke, "Ciceronian Oratory," *G&R* 14(1945)72-81, discusses more general characteristics of Cicero's oratory, including learning, wit, and humor. See also P. Mackendrick, "Cicero's Ideal Orator: Truth and Propaganda," *CJ* 43(1948)339-47 and K. O. Matier, "Cicero the Orator," *Akroterion* 22(1977)1-10. On the cultural ramifications of Cicero's treatises see R. Valenti Pagnini, "La retorica di Cicerone nella moderna problematica culturale," *Bollettino di Studi Latini* 7(1977)327-42; A. Michel, *Rhétorique et philosophie chez Cicéron* (Paris: Presses Universitaires de France, 1960) and "La théorie de la rhétorique chez Cicéron: Eloquence et philosophie," in *Eloquence et rhétorique chez Cicéron*, ed. W. Ludwig, Fondation Hardt, 28 (Geneva: Vandoeuvres, 1982), pp. 109-139; and M. Rambaud, *Cicéron et l'histoire romaine* (Paris: Belles Lettres, 1953).

10. *De inv.* 1.2. Text is from the 1965 Teubner edition, ed. E. Stroebel. Translations are my own.

11. On the beginning of the *De Inventione* and its sources see F. Solmsen, "Drei Rekonstruktionen zur antiken Rhetorik und Poetik," *Hermes* 67(1932)133-54; G. Nuchelmans, "Philologie et son mariage avec Mercurie jusqu'à la fin du XIIe siècle," *Latomus* 16(1957)84-107; and P. Giuffrida, "I due proemi del *De inventione* (I, 1-4,5; II, 1-3,10)," *Miscellanea Terzaghi*, (1963)113-216.

12. "ac mihi quidem videntur homines, cum multis rebus humiliores et infirmiores sint, hac re maxime bestiis praestare, quod loqui possunt" ("It seems to me that man, who is in so many ways less sophisticated and weaker than animals, in this thing stands out most as better among the animals: that he can talk") (*De inv.* 1.4.17).

13. "quare praeclarum mihi quiddam videtur adeptus is, qui, qua re homines bestiis praestent, ea in re hominibus ipsis antecellat" ("Therefore that man seems to me outstanding who excels among men in the same capacity that men stand out among beasts ") (*De inv.* 1.4.21).

14. While arguing from a slightly different tack, J. M. May ("The Rhetoric of Advocacy and Patron-Client Identification: Variation on a Theme," *AJP* 102[1981]308-15) gives a clear account of the relationship asserted between speaker and audience. He cites as well G. Kennedy, "The Rhetoric of Advocacy in Greece and Rome," *AJP* 89(1968)419-36. See also J. Lucas, "La relation de Cicéron à son public," in *Ciceroniana*, ed. A. Michel and R. Verdiere (Leiden: Brill, 1975), pp. 150-59.

15. *De caelo* 268b-69b.

16. *De caelo* 269b-70b.

17. *De physica* 259a-60a.

18. I use the word *humanist* here and elsewhere to refer to the branch of classical rhetoric in which the good is associated with the eloquent.

19. *De physica* 213a–216b.

20. See A. Michel, "L'humanisme cicéronien et la fin de la République," *Rome et nous* (Paris: Picard, 1977), pp. 89–104, and A. Desmouliez, *Cicéron et son goût: Essai sur une définition d'une esthétique romaine à la fin de la République*, Collection Latomus, 150 (Brussels: Latomus, 1976).

21. So J. Solodow reiterates in "Ovid's *Ars amatoria*: The Lover as Cultural Ideal," *Wiener Studien* 90(1977)106–27, esp. pp. 111–12.

22. See, e.g., *De inv.* 1.2.3.

23. *De inv.* 1.2.2.

24. G. Highet, *Speeches in the "Aeneid"* (Princeton: Princeton University Press, 1972). Highet also reminds us that Macrobius (*Saturnalia* 5) says Vergil was as much an orator as a poet, and that P. Annius Florus poses the often repeated question, "Virgilius poeta an rhetor?" M. L. Clarke, in "Rhetorical Influences in the *Aeneid*," *G&R* 18(1949)14–27, makes the point that in Vergil's "rhetorical age" all poets were trained classically and would of necessity have drawn on topoi and loci; moreover, the audience would likewise expect such rhetorical flourishes.

25. *Aen.* 8.668. See Springer, "Vergil's Voice," esp. p. 56.

Chapter 2. Juno's Desire

1. See above all W. Clausen, "An Interpretation of the *Aeneid*," *Harvard Studies in Classical Philology* 68(1964)139–47; M. C. J. Putnam, *The Poetry of the "Aeneid"* (Cambridge, Mass.: Harvard University Press, 1965); and W. R. Johnson, *Darkness Visible* (Berkeley: University of California Press, 1978). Two groups of essays stand out as exemplary of the kinds of scholarship that this new approach opened up: *Vergil: A Collection of Critical Essays*, ed. Steele Commager (Englewood Cliffs, N.J.: Prentice-Hall, 1966); and volume 14 of *Arethusa* (1981), ed. M. C. J. Putnam, in honor of Vergil's bimillennium. For the more traditional readings of the epic see B. Otis, *Virgil: A Study in Civilized Poetry* (Oxford: Clarendon, 1964); V. Pöschl, *The Art of Vergil: Image and Symbol in the "Aeneid*," trans. G. Seligson (Ann Arbor: University of Michigan Press, 1962); and W. S. Anderson, *The Art of the Aeneid* (Englewood Cliffs, N.J.: Prentice Hall, 1969). See also countless articles, including A. F. Stocker, "Vergil in the Service of Augustus," *Vergilius* 26(1980)1–9; T. Frank, "Augustus, Vergil and the Augustan Elogia," *AJP* 59(1938)91–94; A. Gosling, "The Political Level of the *Aeneid*," *Akroterion* 20(1975)42–45; J. N. Hritzu, "Aeneas: The Noblest of Romans," *CW* 42(1949)178–86; and M. G. Murphy, "Vergil as Propagandist," *CW* 19(1926)169–74.

2. On the state of rhetoric in Vergil's time see G. Highet, *Speeches in the "Aeneid"* (Princeton: Princeton University Press, 1972), chap. 1; G. A.

Kennedy, *Classical Rhetoric and Its Christian and Secular Traditions from Ancient to Modern Times* (Chapel Hill: University of North Carolina Press, 1980), chap. 6; M. L. Clarke, "Rhetorical Influences in the *Aeneid*," *G&R* 18(1949)14-27, who notes that Vergil belonged to a rhetorical age and was consequently conscious of his audience; L. A. Springer, "Vergil's Voice of Protest," *CW* 47(1953)55–57: "The benefits of reason and persuasion are noted throughout the *Aeneid*" (p. 55); and V. M. Smirin, "Roman School Rhetoric in the Augustan Age as Historical Source Material," *Vestnik Drevnej Istorii* 139(1977)95-113 (in Russian, with summary on p. 113).

3. Putnam, *Poetry*, passim, esp. pp. 112-17; Johnson, *Darkness*, chap. 3, part 5; see also F. Della Corte, "L'action de Junon dans l'*Enéide*," *Bullétin de l'Association Guillaume Budé,* 1980, 49-58, who argues that the death of Turnus is both the end of the text and the end of Juno; W. S. Anderson, "Juno and Saturn in the *Aeneid*," *Studies in Philology* 55(1958)519-32, states that "until the end of the epic, Juno acts the part of resistance, refusing to change or compromise, furiously attempting by every means at her disposal to maintain conditions as they are" (p. 524). See also J. W. Hunt, *Forms of Glory: Structure and Sense in Virgil's Aeneid* (Southern Illinois Press, 1973), p. 28.

4. That Vergil's Juno is different from other depictions of her, and so both stands out and stands for something new and important, has been recognized by C. W. Amerasinghe, "Saturnia Juno," *G&R* 22 (1953)61-69. The author points out that Vergil's Juno differs from Homer's Hera even though other gods and goddesses (e.g., Venus and Aphrodite) remain the same. While I do not agree with the author's sketch of Juno's career and purpose in the text, I agree with this initial point.

5. While many critics recognize this antiepic strain—what E. A. Hahn calls Vergil's support of the underdog—few have tried to reason what such an emphasis means, whence it is derived, or where it leads. See E. A. Hahn, "Vergil and the Under-Dog," *TAPA* 56(1925)185-212, and Springer, "Vergil's Voice."

6. See R. Coleman, "The Gods in the *Aeneid*," *G&R*, 2d ser. 29(1982)143-68.

7. *De inv.* 2.1.9.

8. *De arch.* 7.5.1. Text from Vitruv, *Zehn Bücher über Architektur*, ed., trans. C. Fensterbusch (Darmstadt: Wissenschaftliche Buchgesellschaft, 1964). Interpolations those of Fensterbusch. The Italian edition by Silvius Ferri, while a less reliable text, has very useful notes. See also A. Novara, "Les raisons d'écrire de Vitruve ou la revanche de l'architecte," *Bullétin de l'Association Guillaume Budé,* 1983, pp. 284–308.

9. *De arch,* 7.5.3,4.

10. This temple was first considered of interest as an architectural curiosity: so G. M. Falion, "The Arts in the *Aeneid* 1-6," *CW* 18(1925)182-86; C. C. van Essen, "L'architecture dans l'*Enéide* de Virgile," *Mnemosyne*, 3d ser. 7(1939)225-36; R. D. Williams, "The Pictures on Dido's Temple (Aeneid 1. 450–93)," *CQ* n.s. 10(1960)145-51. More

recently, however, it has been studied as a metapoetic commentary on the text as a whole: Johnson, *Darkness*, pp. 99-105; J. Romeuf, "Les peintures du temple de Carthage," *Annales Latini Montium Arvenorum* 2(1975)15-27; C. Segal, "Art and the Hero: Participation, Detachment and Narrative Point of View in *Aeneid* I," *Arethusa* 14(1981)67-83. Segal notes that the temple insists on the "necessity of violence, pain and sacrifice."

11. According to H. F. Rebert ("The Felicity of Infelix in Virgil's *Aeneid*," *TAPA* 59[1928]57-71), *infelix* is used a limited number of times in the text, always to refer to a person characterized, like Dido and Troilus, by "irrevocable doom"; it is used most often of Dido.

12. Her "striking" characteristics have elicited censure and support through the ages. That she is a popular character can be surmised from such surveys as the following: P. Considine, "The Sources of the Dido Story in Virgil's *Aeneid*," *Nigeria and the Classics*, n.s. 5 (1961) 53-73; M.-M. Odgers, "Some Appearances of the Dido Story," *CW* 18(1925)145-48; and S. G. Farron, "Dido as Seen by Readers from the Augustans to the Nineteenth Century," *Akroterion* 24(1979)8-13 (favorable views predominate). Essentially the critique of her role falls into two camps: (1) She plays a positive function in acknowledging, however briefly, Aeneas' (or at least Vergil's) humanity—so A. S. Pease, "Some Aspects of the Character of Dido," *CJ* 22(1927)243-52 ("passionately human"); V. B. Evans, "A Study of Dido and Aeneas," *CJ* 33(1937)99-104 (notes her humanity); and P. du Bois, "The *Pharmakos* of Virgil: Dido as Scapegoat," *Vergilius* 22(1976)14-23. See also H. M. Currie, "Dido: Pietas and Pudor," *CB* 51(1975)37-39, and S. F. de Vries and S. Thom, "Suicide of Dido," *Akroterion* 24(1979)14-17. (2) She plays a negative role as sinful temptress of Aeneas and his mission to found Rome—so M. B. Ogle, "Vergil's Conception of Dido's Character," *CJ* 20(1924-25)261-70; W. H. Semple, "Aeneas at Carthage: A Short Study of *Aeneid* I and IV," *Bulletin of the John Rylands Library* 34(1951-52)119-36; S. G. Farron, "The Aeneas-Dido Episode as an Attack on Aeneas's Mission and Rome," *G&R*, 2d ser. 27(1980)34-47; and R. C. Monti, *The Dido Episode and the "Aeneid": Roman Society and Political Values in the Epic, Mnemosyne* supp. 66 (Leiden: Brill, 1981).

13.   regina ad templum, forma pulcherrima Dido
        incessit magna iuvenum stipante caterva.
        qualis in Eurotae ripis aut per iuga Cynthi
        exercet Diana choros, quam mille secutae
        hinc atque hinc glomerantur Oreades; illa pharetram
        fert umero gradiensque deas supereminet omnis. . .
        talis erat Dido.

the queen arrived at the temple, most beautiful Dido, accompanied by a great crowd of youths. Just as on the shores of the Eurotas or through the Cynthian range Diana runs with her dancers, a thousand followers, nymphs that gather around her; she bears a quiver on her shoulder and, walking, shines above all other goddesses. . .so was Dido. (Aen. 1.496-501;503-4).)

14. She is perhaps best characterized by the phrase used of her later, *more ferae*. As N.-W. DeWitt has pointed out in "*Aeneid* IV:551: More Ferae" (*AJP* 45 [1924]176-78), the word *fera* indicated the Roman concept of the cult of virginity and the pride of the outlaw—both of which were certainly true of Dido at least at the time of Aeneas' arrival in Carthage.

15. Interestingly enough, Dido, like Juno, is given a treatment that is unique to Vergil. So T. B. Degraff, "Dido—tota Vergiliana," *CW* 43(1950)147-51.

16. A fascinating diagram at the back of A. Schmitz, *Infelix Dido* (Gembloux: Duculot, 1960), charts through the use of quotations Dido's "psychic reflections." Through this one can see the development of her "illness" and its apparent corollary, her inability to speak.

17. So Cicero: "cum autem res ab nostra memoria propter vetustatem remotas ex litterarum monumentis repetere instituo, multas urbes constitutas, plurima bella restincta, firmissimas societates, sanctissimas amicitias intellego cum animi ratione tum facilius eloquentia comparatas" ("When, however, I start to search for things distant from our own memory in works of literature I find many cities were built, many wars put out, strongest social bonds and most holy friendships formed indeed with the faculty of reason but even more readily with eloquence" (*De inv.* 1.1.7.).

18. So C. Collard, "Medea and Dido," *Prometheus* 1(1975)131-51.

19. Bernard Knox traces Vergil's use of the flame as image in "The Serpent and the Flame: The Imagery of the Second Book of the *Aeneid*," *AJP* 71(1950)379-400; rpt. in *Vergil: A Collection of Critical Essays*, ed. Commager. While Knox refers specifically to the use of such imagery in the second book, a similar approach could be applied to the fourth book and the occurrence of the image in relation to Dido.

20. *De arch.* 2.1.1. Interpolation and emendation that of Fensterbusch.

21. *De arch.* 2.1.2.

22. See M. C. J. Putnam, "*Aeneid* 7 and the *Aeneid*," *AJP* 91(1970)408-30; rpt. in his *Essays on Latin Lyric, Elegy, and Epic* (Princeton: Princeton University Press, 1982), pp. 288-310. See also his *Poetry*, p. 87.

23. Such a use of this ekphrasis has also been suggested by V. Pöschl, "Die Tempeltüren des Dädalus in der *Aeneis* (VI, 14-33)," *Würzburger Jahrbücher für die Altertumswissenschaft* n.s. 1(1975)119-23.

24. Similarly, perhaps, the bulk of book 6 represents Aeneas treading the winding labyrinth of the underworld and, most strikingly, avoiding its version of the Minotaur: Tartarus (*Aen.* 6.540 ff.).

25. The fact that Aeneas rewrites rather than repeats the Icarus myth was pointed out to me by Jessica Riskin, a student in my freshman seminar at Harvard University, Fall 1984.

26. The correspondence between these two scenes has been recognized and discussed by many. See Johnson, *Darkness*, pp. 114ff.; E. L. Highbarger, "The Tragedy of Turnus," *CW* 41(1948)114-24; and T. Van Nortwick, "Aeneas, Turnus and Achilles," *TAPA* 110(1980)303-14. See also W. S. Anderson, "Vergil's Second *Iliad*," *TAPA* 88(1957)17-30 and his *Art of the Aeneid*, chap. 3; L. A. MacKay, "Achilles as Model for Aeneas," *TAPA* 88(1975)11-16; A. Thornton,

"The Last Scene of the *Aeneid*," *G&R* 22(1953)82–84; K. Gransden, *Vergil's "Iliad"* (Cambridge: Cambridge University Press, 1984); and D. West, "The Deaths of Hector and Turnus," *G&R*, 2d. ser. 21(1974)21–31.

27. The moral issue of Aeneas' actions at the end of the text are considered most extensively by Putnam, *Poetry*, chap. 4. See also Johnson, *Darkness*, pp. 114ff.; A. H. F. Thornton, "The Last Scene of the *Aeneid*," *G&R* 22(1953)82–84; W. H. Semple, "The Conclusion of Vergil's *Aeneid*," *Bulletin of the John Rylands Library* 42(1959–60)175–93; G. E. Dimock, "The Mistake of Aeneas," *Yale Review* n.s. 64(1975)334–56; H. P. Stahl, "Aeneas as Unheroic Hero?" *Arethusa* 14(1981)157–77; J. B. Garstang, "The Tragedy of Turnus," *Phoenix* 4(1950)47–58; M. A. Di Cesare, "Contrasting Patterns in Epic: Notes on Aeneas and Turnus," *Classica et Mediaevalia* 30(1969)308–20; and Anderson, *Art,* chap. 7.

28. The problem of the last line has been deliberated by many, as the text ends very abruptly. Scholars have questioned whether the issues of the work are resolved, whether the work is really finished, and just what the intent of the last line is. See E. N. Genovese, "Deaths in the *Aeneid*," *Pacific Coast Philology* 10(1975)22–28, who notes that the "*Aeneid* must be resolved not simply at its end with the death of Turnus, but in the deliberate, progressive elimination of Turnus's furious prefigurements" (p. 26). E. D. Daniels, in "Ultima Verba" (*CW* 23[1930]173–74), notes the abrupt quality of the ending and suggests that "several more lines should have been added to show how these ends [the purpose of the text] had been achieved or were to be achieved."

29. This fact has been noted by others, including Putnam, *Poetry*, p. 156. Many others note in passing a similarity between Camilla and Turnus—so E. A. Hahn, "Vergil and the Under-Dog," comments that they both bring about their own downfalls because of their similar moral corruption of arrogance and violence (pp. 205–6). In line with this, it is interesting to note that Dante places Turnus with Camilla in *Inferno* 1.

30. The role of women in the *Aeneid* is particularly problematical, as Vergil's attitude is not at all consistent. Dido seems to receive special treatment because she spans the spectrum of human possibility—she shifts from the personification of reason to that of passion. The other women receive a much shallower consideration, yet one that is nonetheless instructive. On women in the *Aeneid* see A. Flotteron, *La donna e la poesia virgiliana* (Napoli: Chiurazzi, 1931); and G. S. West, "Women in Vergil's *Aeneid*" (diss., University of California at Los Angeles, 1975).

31. On Amata see P. F. Burke, "Virgil's Amata," *Vergilius* 22(1976)24–29 and S. Patris, "Une figure féminine de l'*Enéide:* Amata, reine des Latins," *Etudes Classiques* 13(1945)40–54.

32. In "Did Virgil Fail?" (*Cicero and Virgil: Studies in Honor of Harold Hunt,* ed. J. R. C. Martyn [Amsterdam: Hakkert, 1972], pp. 192–206), Kenneth Quinn suggests that Vergil wrote the last, Iliadic half of the *Aeneid* first. If this is so, then book 7 becomes even more important to the argument, as the emphasis on the defining role of women would

have been given primary importance.

33. Undoubtedly the most influential piece written on Camilla is E. Auerbach's chapter "Camilla; or, The Rebirth of the Sublime," in his *Literary Language and Its Public in Late Latin Antiquity and in the Middle Ages*, trans. R. Manheim (New York: Pantheon, 1965), chap. 3. More recently, however, G. Arrigoni has written a fascinating monograph on the mythic and anthropological sources of the character of Camilla: *Camilla: Amazzone e sacerdotessa di Diana*, Testi e documenti per lo studio dell'antichità 69 (1982). See also P. Faider, "Camille (*Enéide* VII, 803–12; IX, 498–915)," *Revue des Philologies Classiques* 34(1930)59–81; G. S. West, "Chloreus and Camilla," *Vergilius* 31(1985)22–29; and N.-W. DeWitt, "Vergil's Tragedy of Maidenhood," *CW* 18(1924–25)107–8. DeWitt's opinion is that Vergil's depiction of Camilla is "too slight." She is a gem, a cameo, "as if done in hard material." He also makes the point that her murder marks a difference between her and Dido. While I agree that her story is not identical to that of Dido, I think hers is a valorized rewriting of the Dido story, and more alike than different. There is suggestive evidence to support this: Camilla's confidante is named Acca, Dido's Anna; Camilla is released by Opis, Dido by Iris.

34. *Servii Grammatici Commentarii*, ed. G. Thilo, vol. 2 (Hildesheim, 1887), on book 11, line 588.

35. Macrobius, *Saturnalia* 3.8.7, ed. J. Willis (Leipzig: Teubner, 1963).

36. See N. Brown, *Hermes the Thief* (New York: Random House, 1947).

37. In fact, the connections between the two are explicitly made, especially in the later books. See Pöschl, *Art*, pp. 167–68; for differences, see Di Cesare, "Contrasting Patterns."

38. Basic background on Vergil's fourth Eclogue can be found in M. C. J. Putnam, *Virgil's Pastoral Art* (Princeton: Princeton University Press, 1970), chap. 3. See also C. Brakman, "Ad Vergilii Eclogam quartam," *Mnemosyne* n.s. 54(1926)10–18 and R. G. Austin, "Virgil and the Sibyl," *CQ* 21(1927)100–105.

39. That the fourth Eclogue was to some degree prophetic is discussed by Carcopino, *Virgile et le mystère de la IVe Eclogue* (Paris: L'Artisan du Livre, 1930), and A. Vaccari, "Il messianismo ebraico e la IV Egloga di Virgilio," *Civiltà Cattolica* 2(1851)3–20, 96–107. The specifically Christian tradition to which it belongs is discussed in P. Courcelle, "Les exégèses chrétiennes de la quatrième Eglogue," *Revue des Etudes anciennes* 59(1957)294–319, and A. Kurfess, "Ad Vergilii eclogae IV versionem graecam," *Philologische Wochenschrift* 56(1936)364–67 (Greek version for Constantine).

Chapter 3.   Augustine and the Reincorporation of Desire

1. Text from CSEL 33, pp. 24–25; the translation is by R. S. Pine-Coffin (New York: Penguin, 1961).

2. Vergil had a tremendous effect on Augustine, which is acknowledged by practically everyone who writes on him. "That the *Aeneid* was the book of all others that affectand [sic] was loved by the growing Augustine is beyond question" (J. O'Meara, "Augustine the Artist and the *Aeneid*," *Mélanges Mohrmann* [Utrecht-Awens: Spectrum 1963], p. 257). O'Meara's article is by far the most insightful on the profound creative influence that Vergil had on Augustine. A short list of others who acknowledge such influence follows: H. Hagendahl, *Augustine and the Latin Classics* (Goteburg: Elanders Boktryckeri Aktiebolag, 1967), vol. 2, chap. 2, pp. 384-463; H.-I. Marrou, *Saint Augustin et la fin de la culture antique* (Paris: E. de Boccard, 1938); H. C. Coffin, "The Influence of Virgil on St. Jerome and on St. Augustine," *CW* 17(1923)170-75; D. Bassi, "Sant'Agostino e Virgilio," *Annale dell'Istruzione Media* 6(1930)420-31, points out that Augustine loved and studied Vergil, cited him 108 times, and saw him as a poet who conquered pagan idolatry in hopes of the coming redemption. A number of articles are useful for their gathering of Augustine's pagan sources: for example, P. Courcelle, "La suivie littéraire de l'*Enéide*," *Annuaire du Collège de France* 80(1979-80)681-93, and J. J. O'Donnell, "Augustine's Classical Readings," *Recherches Augustiniennes* 15(1980) 144-75. Other related texts are cited below in reference to the influence of classical rhetoric on Augustine.

3. So, e.g., O'Meara, *Mélanges Mohrmann*, who points out an additional parallel between Augustine's leaving Monica and Theseus' leaving Ariadne (p. 260).

4. So C. Collard, "Medea and Dido," *Prometheus* 1(1975)131-51.

5. This is especially striking when considered against the backdrop of the ekphrasis in *Aeneid* 6. There, as pointed out in the last chapter, the story of Ariadne and Theseus is supplemented by the story of Daedalus and Icarus. By suggesting that Aeneas, at the end of the *Aeneid*, is a new Icarus and that the new Icarus is also Medea, Augustine is merely finishing the equation Vergil had to leave undone.

6. Whether the *Confessions* is solely an autobiography has been seriously questioned by E. Vance, "The Functions and Limits of Autobiography in Augustine's *Confessions*," *Poetics Today* 5(1984)399-409, and "Augustine's Confessions and the Grammar of Selfhood," *Genre* 6(1973)1-28. See also Peter Brown, *Saint Augustine: A Biography* (London: Faber and Faber, 1967); P. Grant, "Redeeming the Time: The Confessions of Saint Augustine," *By Things Seen*, ed. D. L. Jeffrey (Ottawa: University of Ottawa Press, 1979), pp. 21-32. While the *De doctrina* has for some time been recognized as a handbook to Christian culture (see E. Kevane, "Augustine's *De Doctrina Christiana*: A Treatise on Christian Education," *Recherches Augustiniennes* 4[1966]97-133) and not just as a rhetorical treatise, the *Confessions* is only recently being interpreted in this broader way.

7. The influence of Cicero on Augustine is most commonly discussed in relation to the *De doctrina christiana*, where Augustine himself mentions Cicero. Yet the influence is no less evident in the *Confessions*, especially if we view Cicero's rhetoric as the societal model. On

Cicero's influence on Augustine see, above all, E. L. Fortin, "Augustine and the Problem of Christian Rhetoric," *AugStud* 5(1974)85-100, and the series of articles by J. Oròz: "Hacia una retórica cristiana: San Agustin y Cicero," *Augustinus* 7(1962)77-88; "San Agustin y la cultura clásica," *Helmantica* 14(1963)79-166, rpt. in *Augustinus* 8(1963)5-20; and "El doctrina cristiana o la retórica cristiana," *Estudios Clásicos* 3(1956)452-59. Also useful are C. S. Baldwin, "St. Augustine and the Rhetoric of Cicero," *Proceedings of the Classical Association* 22(1952)24-46; J. J. Murphy, "St. Augustine and the Debate about Christian Rhetoric," *Quarterly Journal of Speech* 46(1960)400-410; Louis D. McNew, "The Relation of Cicero's Rhetoric to Augustine," *Research Studies of the State College of Washington* 25(1957)5-13; and F. Jansen, "Saint Augustin et la Rhétorique," *Nouvelle Revue Théologique* 57(1930)282-97. See also F. Walter, "Zu Cicero und Augustinus," *Philologische Wochenschrift* 61(1941)431-32; P. Cherchi, "Un'eco ciceroniana in S. Agostino," *RevEtAug* 19(1973)303-4; U. Mariani, "San Agostino: Oratore e scrittore," *Augustiniana* 5(1955)121-40; W. H. Semple, "Augustine Rhetor," *Journal of Ecclesiastical History* 1(1950)135-50; J. Kopperschmidt, "Rhetorik und Theodizee: Studie zur hermeneutischen Funktionalität der Rhetorik bei Augustin," *Kerygma und Dogma* 17(1971)273-91; W. Schmidt-Dengler, "Der rhetorische Aufbau des achten Buches der *Konfessionen* des heiligen Augustin," *RevEtAug* 15(1969)195-208; J. Garcia Jimenez, "La retórica de San Agustin y su patrimonio clásico," *Ciudad de Dios* 178(1955)11-32; and A. Michel, "Dialogue philosophique et vie intérieure: Cicéron, Sénèque, Saint Augustin," *Helmantica* 28(1977)353-76. See also W. Schmid, "Il problema della valutazione di Cicerone nelle *Confessione* di San Agostino," in *Scritti in onore di G. Perrotta*, ed. B. Gentili (Urbino: Università degli studi di Urbino, 1965), pp. 207-14, and C. Mohrmann, "St. Augustine and the *Eloquentia*," in *Etudes sur le latin des chrétiens*, (Rome: Edizione di Storia e Letteratura 1961) vol. 1, pp. 351-70.

8. The most useful general book in English on the catacombs is J. Stevenson, *The Catacombs* (London: Thames and Hudson, 1978). See also J. Wilpert, *Roma sotteranea: Die Malereien der Katakomben Romes* (Freiburg-im-Breisgau: Herder, 1903); O. Marucchi, *Le catacombe romane* (Rome: La Libreria dello Stato, 1932); G. B. de Rossi, *La Roma sotteranea cristiana* (Rome: Cromolitografia Pontificia, 1964); P. Testini, *Archeologia cristiana* (Rome: Desclée, 1958); and, W. Tronzo's new book on the Via Latina catacomb, cited in note 48.

9. Jerome, *Comm. in Ezech.*, 40.5, Bk. 12 (PL 25, cols. 375 A-B). Translation from Stevenson, *The Catacombs*, p. 24.

10. See G. Gassiot-Talabot, *La peinture romaine et paléochrétienne* (Lausanne: Editions Rencontre, 1965). Compare, for instance, the painting in the houses under San Sebastiano with the catacomb paintings adjacent, or the paintings from the catacombs at Domitilla with the Casa des Noces at Pompeii. See also the paintings at Ostia, and the experimentation with illusionism done in several of the catacombs such as the Hypogeum of the Aurelii and the Via Latina. For the origins of this

style and its roots in pagan painting, see H. Joyce, *The Decoration of Walls, Ceilings, and Floors in Italy in the Second and Third Centuries* (Rome: Bretschneider, 1981); M. I. Rostovtzeff, "Ancient Decorative Wall-Painting," *Journal of Hellenic Studies* 39(1919)144-63; H. Brandenburg, "Überlegungen zum Ursprung der frühchristlichen Bildkunst" (*Atti* 9), *Studi di antichità cristiana* 32(1978)331-60; and L. De Bruyne, "L'importanza degli scavi Lateranensi per la cronologia delle prime pitture catacombali," *RAC* 44(1968)81-113.

11. See A. Nestori, *Repertorio topografico delle pitture delle catacombe romane* (Città del Vaticano: PIAC, 1975). The choice of scenes painted in the catacombs has been ascribed to the liturgy of the dead. While indeed many of the repeated scenes do occur in this liturgy, none of the extant copies dates from this period. Moreover, this source does not account fully for the arrangement of scenes as discussed below. So A.-G. Martimort, "L'iconographie des catacombes et la catéchèse antique," *RAC* 25(1949)105-14; P. du Bourguet, "Le sujet figuratif et la valeur qu'il revêt dans les monuments préconstantiniens," (*Atti* 9) *Studi di antichità cristiana* 32(1978), 383-89; G. J. Hoogewerf, "L'iconologie et son importance pour l'étude systématique de l'art chrétien," *RAC* 8(1931)53-85; G. Bovini, "Monumenti tipici del linguaggio figurative della pittura cimiteriale d'età paleocristiana," *Corsi di cultura sull'arte ravennate e bizantina* (Ravenna: Longo, 1957), fasc. 1; G. P. Kirsch, "Sull'origine dei motivi iconografici nella pittura cimiteriale di Roma," *RAC* 4(1927)254-87; and A. Grabar, "Plotin et les origines de l'esthétique médiévale," *Cahiers Archéologiques* 1(1945)15-34.

12. A. Grabar, *Christian Iconography: A Study of its Origins*, Bollingen Series, 35.10 (Princeton: Princeton University Press, 1968).

13. L. De Bruyne has proposed an ambitious program for understanding the organization of scenes in the catacombs. In "Les 'lois' de l'art paléochrétienne comme instrument herméneutique" (*RAC* 35[1959]105-86, 39[1963]7-92), De Bruyne speaks of the figurative language of the catacombs and argues, very persuasively, that it is extremely important to decode this arrangement of the particular scenes chosen as it is this organization that transmits a particular Christian message. This extensive piece develops a Christian tropology for the catacomb paintings based on such factors as symmetry, juxtaposition, antithesis, rhythm, and interruption by insertion. Following a similarly rhetorical line is the series of arguments by A. Quacquarelli, most notably in his *Retorica e iconologia* (Bari: Istituto di Letteratura Cristiana Antica, 1982) and his earlier articles, including "Inventio ed elocutio nella retorica cristiana antica," *Vetus Christianorum* 9(1972)191-218, and "L'antitesi retoricam," *Vetus Christianorum* 19(1982)223-37. I am much indebted to De Bruyne and Quacquarelli in the argument that follows. See also E. Kitzinger, *Early Medieval Art with Illustrations from the British Museum Collection* (Bloomington: Indiana University Press, 1940).

14. It should be noted that the identification of this figure with the term *orans* is a nineteenth-century construct. See H.-I. Marrou, *Décadence Romaine ou Antiquité tardive?* (*IIIe–IVe siècle*) (Paris: Editions du Seuil,

1977), p. 58, and G. de St-Laurent, "Nouveaux éclaircissements sur l'orante," *RAC* 10(1879)120–70.

15. Hilary, *Comm. in Matt.* 5 (PL 9, 942–43); *Psalm* CXL (PL 9, 824–25; 639–42); Ambrose (PL 14, 307); Lactantius, *Div. Inst.* 1.1, 2.1, 5.1 (PL 6, 549).

16. So J. Quasten, *Patrology* (Utrecht: Spectrum, 1950), vol. 1, pp. 118–22. Mentioned by Origen, Clement, and Justin Martyr, there were three hundred manuscripts of the *Protevangelium* by the fourth century, and it was translated by Jerome, among others.

17. *Apocryphal Gospels*, Ante-Nicene Christian Fathers Library, 16, ed. and trans. A. Walker (Edinburgh, 1870), p. 11. There are newer translations, one by A. J. B. Higgins (Philadelphia: Westminster, 1963), the other by M. R. James (Oxford: Clarendon, 1964), but they read less well than the one cited here. The passage commented on here is assumed by some to be interpolated, as it does not appear in the oldest manuscript.

18. So C. Dagens, "A propos du cubiculum de la Vélatio," *RAC* 47(1971)119–31. But see K. Pfister, *Katakomben Malerei* (Potsdam: Gustav Kiepenheuer, 1924).

19. Vat. Lat. 5409 f.16r.

20. The relation between early Christian art and the Fathers is problematical at best. E. Kirschbaum, "Monumenti e letteratura nell'iconografia paleocristiana," (*Atti* 6), *Studi di antichità cristiana* 26(1965) 741–49, says it is important to know the Fathers to understand the catacombs, while A. Stuiber, *Refrigerium interim* (Bonn: P. Hanstein 1957), says they are not the answer. P. Corby Finney, "Gnostics and the Origins of Early Christian Art," (*Atti* 9), *Studi di antichità cristiana* 32(1978) 391–405, draws a connection between Gnosticism and images in early Christian art, mentioning Irenaeus, *Adv. haer.* 1.25.6. See also D. Iturgaiz, "Arte cristiano y literatura patristica," *Apuntes para una iconografía paleocristiana y bizantina* 19(1978)157–227.

21. Clement of Alexandria, *Miscellanies*, book 9, chap. 9, in *The Ante-Nicene Christian Fathers*, ed. A. Roberts and J. Donaldson (Grand Rapids, Mich.: Eerdmans, 1979), vol. 2, pp. 457–58.

22. The best survey of these scenes is by C. Carletti, *I tre giovani ebrei di Babilonia nell'arte cristiana antica* (Brescia: Paideia, 1975).

23. The same trend can be detected in other aspects of fourth-century Roman Christian art. In much of the Christian art of this period, verbal as well as visual, pagan methods were being reintroduced, particularly those methods of Republican and Augustan Rome. Much of fourth-century literature echoes Augustan literature: Sedulius writes a "Carmen de Incarnatione" (Cento Virgilianus), Optatian writes one poem that echoes the Eclogues and the *Aeneid*, and another (the *Triumphus Christi Heroicus*) that recalls Vergil's style in its syntax and lexicon. Others echo Catullus. In addition there are numerous songs to Constantine in which he is referred to as Augustus or *pius* Augustus; while the term *augustus* was originally only an honorific, its use by Octavian had virtually changed it from an adjective to a proper noun, and its use in conjunction with *pius* only reinforced the

connection to the emperor. Constantine is viewed, it would appear, as a second Augustus, the true Augustus who is truly pious and who reigns over the true Golden Age. While the content of all these poems has been ostensibly Christianized, the forms—terms, phrases, and so on—are largely Augustan. See *The Conflict between Paganism and Christianity in the Fourth Century*, ed. A. Momigliano (Oxford: Clarendon, 1963); Y.-M. Duval, "Formes profanes et formes bibliques dans les oraisons funèbres de S. Ambrose," in *Christianisme et formes littéraires de l'antiquité tardive en Occident*, ed. M. Fuhrmann (Geneva: Vandoeuvres, 1977), pp. 235-91, who finds a conscious adaptation of classical rules of rhetoric together with a stated rejection of pagan rules; and J. Fontaine ("Unité et diversité du mélange des genres et des tons chez quelques écrivains latins de la fin du IVe siècle: Ausone, Ambroise, Ammien," pp. 425-72 of the same volume) who sees more similarity with pagan practice than difference. A. Cameron ("Paganism and Literature in Late Fourth-Century Rome," pp. 1-30 of the same volume) disagrees, arguing that such pagan reaction as occurred in the fourth century was largely due to apathy.

The visual arts show a similar classicizing tendency. The best example of this, as I. Lavin has shown, is provided by the ceiling frescoes at Trier, a basilica built by Constantine. Lavin, "The Ceiling Frescoes in Trier and Illusionism in Constantinian Painting," *Dumbarton Oaks Papers* 21(1967)99-113, argues that the painting does not attempt to create the illusion of "space receding beyond limits" (as Roman art had continued to do) but instead appears as a somewhat anachronistic attempt to use the wall as the limit of the room. Lavin feels that this style is a "violent rejection" of third-century linear style in Rome that suggests affinities with the early style of Pompeii. While Lavin feels that this fourth-century style represents a progressive development from later Pompeian style rather than a regressive reaction, the fact remains that here too, as with the literature, earlier pagan influences resurface in the style of the most Christian art of the period, and, most important for our purposes, the particular influence felt is that of a pagan Augustan style. See also E. Kitzinger, "A Marble Relief of the Theodosian Period," *Dumbarton Oaks Papers* 14(1960)19-42, and S. Pelekanidis, "Gli affreschi paleocristiana ed i piu antichi mosaici parietali de Salonicco," *Collana di quaderni di Antichità Ravennati* 2(1963)7-60.

24. For a fuller discussion of Augustine's authority as rhetor, see R. Flores, *The Rhetoric of Doubtful Authority: Deconstructive Readings of Self-Questioning Narratives, St. Augustine to Faulkner* (Ithaca: Cornell University Press, 1984), chap. 2, "Doubling-Making St. Augustine's *Confessions*."

25. CSEL 77.

26. See J. Rieck, "*De Magistro* and Augustine's Illumination Theory," *Reality* 12(1964)95-115; P. H. Baker, "Liberal Arts as Philosophical Liberation: St. Augustine's *De Magistro*," *Arts libéraux et philosophie au Moyen-Age* (Montreal/Paris: Vrin, 1969), pp. 469-79; G. Madec, "Analyse du 'De Magistro,'" *RevEtAug* 21(1975)63-71: "The *De*

Magistro is not a dialogue about the impossibility of dialogue, nor about the impossibility of teaching, but rather about the conditions of possibility. If Augustine undoes language by reducing it to its materiality and its exteriority, it is in order to reveal the interiority and profundity of the soul. He aims to dissipate the illusion of a "horizontal communication" among men as a way of convincing them that the only communion among souls is in their union with Truth" (My translation). See also R. Nouilhat, *Le spiritualisme chrétien dans sa constitution: Approche matérialiste des discours d'Augustin* (Paris: Desclée, 1976), pp. 147ff., who shows how the rhetoric of mystery often follows a Ciceronian structure.

27. W. J. O'Brien ("The Liturgical Form of Augustine's Conversion Narrative and Its Theological Significance," *AugStud* 9[1978]45-58) notes that this scene with the pears is structured on a "paradigm of original sin" (p. 57); See also L. C. Ferrari's three articles: "Arboreal polarisation in Augustine's *Confessions*," *RevEtAug* 25(1979)35-46; "Symbols of Sinfulness in Book II of Augustine's *Confessions*," *AugStud* 2(1971)93-104; and "The Pear-Theft in Augustine's Confessions," *RevEtAug* 16(1970)233-42.

28. CSEL 33, p. 36; Pine-Coffin, p. 47.

29. I owe much of the following to K. Burke, *Rhetoric of Religion* (Boston: Beacon, 1961). This remarkable book inspired me to pursue the rhetorical cast I felt to be present in these scenes, in a way that would never have occurred to me on my own. Reinforcement of this approach is offered by F. Van der Meer, *Augustine the Bishop*, trans. B. Battershaw and G. R. Lamb (London: Sheed and Ward, 1961).

30. CSEL 33, p. 193; Pine-Coffin, p. 177.

31. See *De inv.* 1.3.4.

32. CSEL 33, p. 194; Pine-Coffin, p. 178.

33. On this moment of conversion see P. Courcelle, "Source chrétienne et allusions païennes de l'épisode du 'Tolle Lege,'" *Revue d'Histoire et de Philosophie Réligieuses* 32(1952)171-200; L. C. Ferrari, "Ecce audio vocem de vicina domo," *Augustiniana* 33(1983)232-45, and "Paul at the Conversion of Augustine," *AugStud* 11(1980)5-20; L. J. Daly, "Psychohistory and St. Augustine's Conversion Process," *Augustiniana* 28(1978)231-54; P. Sejourne, "Les conversions de Saint Augustin," *Revue des Sciences Réligieuses* 25(1951)243-64, 333-63; and R. Flores, "Reading and Speech in St. Augustine's *Confessions*," *AugStud* 6(1975)1-14.

34. So Burke, *Rhetoric of Religion*, p. 66.

35. These last books, which offer a close reading of the first few lines of Genesis, present a real problem in trying to understand the unity of the text. See M. Colish, *The Mirror of Language* (Lincoln: University of Nebraska Press, 1983), pp. 46-49; also A. Pincherle, "The Confessions of St. Augustine: A Reappraisal," *AugStud* 7(1976)119-33; Vance, *Mervelous Signals,* chap. 1; and J. C. Cooper, "Why Did Augustine Write Books IX-XIII of The Confessions?" *AugStud* 2(1971)37-46.

36. Colish, *The Mirror of Language*, p. 25; see also W. Mallard, "The

Incarnation in Augustine's Conversion," *Recherches Augustiniennes* 15(1980)80–98.

37. It is perhaps significant that Mary is often shown reading.

38. Nouilhat, *Le spiritualisme*, quotes H. de Lubac (*L'écriture dans la tradition*) "The spiritual process is identical, in its structure, to the process of conversion" and then adds: "The function of allegory as a system of ambiguity and the pragmatic aspect that Augustine confers upon it constitutes the intellectual framework for his conversion" (my translation).

39. E. Vance, "Saint Augustine: Language as Temporality," in *Mimesis: From Mirror to Method, Augustine to Descartes*, ed. J. D. Lyons and S. G. Nichols, Jr. (Hanover, N.H.: University Press of New England, 1982), p. 35; rpt. in his *Mervelous Signals: Poetics and Sign Theory in the Middle Ages* (Lincoln: University of Nebraska Press, 1986), chap. 2.

40. Other articles on the vision at Ostia include J. Maréchal, "La vision du Dieu au sommet de la contemplation d'après S.Augustin," *Nouvelle Revue Théologique* 57(1930)89–109, 191–214; A. Faggi, "L'exstasi di Ostia," *Atti della Accademia delle Scienze di Torino* 71(1935-36)213–21; J. Huby, "La vision d'Ostie: Un noeud de rencontre," *Etudes Traditionnelles* 44(1939)782–88; G. St. Hilaire, "The Vision of Ostia: Acquired or Infused?" *Modern Schoolman* 35(1958)117–23; and V. Zangara, "La visione di Ostia," *Rivista di Storia e Letteratura Religiosa* 15(1979)63–82.

41. See also Van der Meer, *Augustine the Bishop*, p. 451; M. Suchocki, "The Symbolic Structure of Augustine's *Confessions*," *Journal of the American Academy of Religion* 50(1982)365–78; and A. D'Ales, "Sur la trace de Saint Augustin," *Etudes Traditionnelles* 35(1930)81–88, who speaks of a mystical order that organizes Augustine's texts.

42. See J. B. Allard, *La nature du De catechizandis rudibus de Saint Augustin* (Rome: Université Latran et Collège Canadien, 1976).

43. *De catechizandis rudibus* 2.3; CC Series Latina 46, p. 122. The translation is mine.

44. On Augustine and Platonism in this context see R. Nash, "St. Augustine on Man's Knowledge of the Forms," *New Scholasticism* 41(1967)223–34, and A. H. Armstrong, "St. Augustine and Christian Platonism," *St. Augustine Lectures*, (Villanova, 1967); rpt. in *Augustine: A Collection of Critical Essays*, ed. R. A. Markus (Garden City, N.Y.: Doubleday-Anchor, 1972), pp. 3–37. See also R. Jolivet, *Essai sur le rapport entre la pensée grecque et la pensée chrétienne* (Paris: Vrin, 1931), and J. Pepin, "Note nouvelle sur le problème de la communication des consciences chez Plotin et Saint Augustin," *Revue des Métaphysiques et de Morale* 56(1951)316–26.

45. Plato, *Phaedrus and the Seventh and Eighth Letters*, trans. W. Hamilton (Harmondsworth: Penguin, 1973), pp. 135, 136. Emendations those of translator. For question of dubious authorship see Hamilton, pp. 105–6. It is also interesting to note that Augustine paraphrases this passage from Plato in *De doctrina christiana* 4.1, where he says that the reader should not expect to learn the rules of rhetoric from him "in this work or in any other."

46. Augustine transmutes this into a trinitarian model in several instances,

suggesting that the divine spark be understood as the Holy Ghost, whom he describes as both a flame and an inner teacher. See *Confessions* 13.9 and *In Johannis Evangelium tractatus* 3,13.

47. Augustine's complex theory of knowledge is beyond the scope of this investigation. What we are concerned with here is the specific relation of language to persuasion, how it affects the dynamics of speaker to audience, and how it reflects a shift in intellectual structure. On the theory of knowledge and illumination the following are very helpful: Marrou, *Saint Augustin*; R. Nash, "Structure of St. Augustine's Theory of Knowledge," *Gordon Review* 8(1964)25-34; R. J. O'Connell, *Art and the Christian Intelligence in St. Augustine* (Cambridge, Mass.: Harvard University Press, 1978); G. Howie, *Educational Theory and Practice in St. Augustine* (New York: Teacher's College Press, 1969), chap. 4, "Intellect and the Quest for Truth"; S. Grabowski, "St. Augustine and the Presence of God," *Theological Studies* 13(1952)336-58; C. Boyer, "Les voies de la connaissance de Dieu selon S. Augustin," *Augustinus* 3(1958)303-07; B. S. Bubacz, "Augustine's Illumination Theory and Epistemic Structuring," *AugStud* 11(1980) 35-48; V. J. Bourke, "Light of Love: Augustine on Moral Illumination," *Medievalia* 4(1978)13-31.

48. See above all W. Tronzo, *The Via Latina Catacomb: Imitation and Discontinuity in Fourth-Century Roman Painting* (State College: Pennsylvania State University Press, 1984); A. Ferrua, *Le pitture della nuova catacombe di Via Latina* (Città del Vaticano: PIAC, 1960); J. Fink, *Hermeneutische Probleme in der Katakombe der Via Latina in Rom*, n.f. 18 *Kairos* (1976)178-90; E. Kirschbaum, "Die neue Katakombe an der Via Latina," *Römische Quartelschrift* 51(1956)127-29; M. Simon, "Remarques sur la catacombe de la Via Latina," *Festschrift Klauser* (Münster-Westfalen: Aschendorffsche Verlagsbuchhandlung, 1964) 327-35; J. Fink, "Lazarus an der Via Latina," *Römische Quartelschrift* 64(1969)209-17; W. N. Schumacher, "Reparatio Vitae: Zum Programm der neuen Katakombe an der Via Latina zu Rom," *Römische Quartelschrift* 66(1971)125-53; L. Kötzsche-Breitenbruch, *Die neue Katakombe an der Via Latina in Rom: Untersuchungen zur Ikonographie der alttestamentliche Wandmalerei* (Münster-Westfalen: Aschendorffsche Verlagsbuchhandlung, 1976).

49. So Ferrua, *Le pitture*, and Kötzsche-Breitenbruch "Die neue Katakombe."

50. R. Brilliant, *Gesture and Rank in Roman Art: The Use of Gesture to Denote Status in Roman Sculpture and Coinage* (New Haven: The Academy, 1963).

51. Clement of Alexandria, *Miscellanies*, book 5, chap. 12, in *The Ante-Nicene Christian Fathers*, pp. 462-63.

52. See G. Press's two articles, which neatly summarize the foregoing critical tradition as prelude to a new reading: "The Subject and Structure of Augustine's De Doctrina Christiana," *AugStud* 11(1980) 99-124, and "The Content and Argument of Augustine's De Doctrina Christiana," *Augustiniana* 31(1981)165-82. See also L. M. J. Verheijen, "Le De Doctrina Christiana de Saint Augustin," *Augustiniana* 24(1974)

10-20; E. Kevane, "Augustine's *De Doctrina Christiana:* A Treatise on Christian Education," *Recherches Augustiniennes* 4(1966)97-133, and, "Paideia and Anti-Paideia: The *Prooemium* of S. Augustine's *De Doctrina Christiana,*" *AugStud* 1(1970)153-70; S. Prete, "Ars rhetorica e cultura cristiana nel De Doctrina Christiana di S. Agostino," *Divus Thomas* 73(1970)59-68; G. Ripanti, "L'allegoria o l'intellectus figuratus nel *De Doctrina Christiana* di Agostino," *RevEtAug* 18(1972)219-32.

53. All quotations from the Latin are taken from CSEL 80, ed. W. M. Green (1963); the English translation is that of D. W. Robertson, Jr., *On Christian Doctrine* (Indianapolis: Bobbs-Merrill, 1958).

54. So Cicero, "partes autem eae [rhetoricae] quas plerique dixerunt, inventio, dispositio, elocutio, memoria, pronuntiatio" ("the parts of [rhetoric] are, as many have said: *inventio, dispositio, elocutio, memoria, pronuntiatio*") (*De inv.* 1.7.9). From the time of the later Cicero (e.g., *De oratore*), however, rhetoric was commonly understood as divided into two major parts, preparation and presentation. These two parts took on various names—invention and elocution, invention and delivery—and it is perhaps from this simplified breakdown that Augustine gets his division into *inveniendo* and *preferendo*.

55. See S. Lanzaro, *Presenza classica e cristiana in San Agostino alla luce del De Doctrina Christiana.* (Napoli: Ferraro, 1974).

56. The rhetoric of the *De doctrina christiana* has been discussed by many. However, discussion usually centers on one of two issues: the three levels of style discussed in book 4 and Augustine's notion of the sign from book 1. See B. D. Jackson, "The Theory of Signs in S. Augustine's *De doctrina christiana,*" *RevEtAug* 15(1969)9-49; D. E. Daniels, "The Argument of the *De Trinitate* and Augustine's Theory of Signs," *AugStud* 8(1977)33-54; G. H. Allard, "L'articulation du sens et du signe dans le *De Doctrina Christiana* de Saint Augustin," *Studia Patristica: Texte und Untersuchungen zur Geschichte der altchristlichen Literatur* 14(1975)377-88; L. G. Kelley, "Saint Augustine and Saussurean Linguistics," *AugStud* 6(1975)45-64. See also M. W. Ferguson, "Saint Augustines's Region of Unlikeness: The Crossing of Exile and Language," *Georgia Review* 29(1975)842-64.

57. That Cicero intended to write a much larger work covering all five parts of rhetoric can be inferred from 2.59.178, where he claims to have written all he can on invention and promises to cover the rest in later books, and from the fact that this work, known commonly as the *De inventione*, was originally entitled *Rhetorici libri*.

58. The original form of the *De doctrina christiana* (started around 396) went only as far as paragraph 35 of book 3. Not until much later (around 427) did Augustine, while writing his *Retractions*, add the rest of book 3 and all of book 4. See F. Cavallera, "La date de la première édition incomplète du *De doctrina christiana,*" *Bullétin de littérature ecclésiastique* 31(1930)122-23.

59. That Augustine's real concern is with the obscure passages of the Scriptures is evident from the layout of the book as a whole. He begins with the simplest issues and progresses to the more complex and significant; he first deals with grammatical impediments and obscuri-

ties and then gives all of his attention in the third book to figural ambiguities: "Therefore, when the reader has been prepared by this instruction so that he is not impeded by unknown signs . . . let him turn next to the examination and consideration of ambiguous signs in the Scriptures, concerning which I shall essay to set forth in the third book . . ." (p. 78).

60. Prol.18; Robertson, p. 7.
61. Prol.19; Robertson, p. 7.
62. So, e.g., 1.17.16; 1.33.36; 3.1.1.
63. 1.82-83; Robertson, pp. 29-30.
64. On charity as an innovative part of rhetoric and prayer, see G. Garcia Montano, "Doctrine agustiniano de la oracìon," *Augustinus* 18(1973) 279-302; L. I. Scipioni, "La caritàs della predicazione nei trattati *De catechizandis rudibus* e *De doctrina christiana* di S.Agostino," *Studi sulla predicazione* 6 (1958)13-30.
65. 3.36; Robertson, p. 88.
66. D. W. Robertson, Jr., *A Preface to Chaucer: Studies in Medieval Perspectives* (Princeton: Princeton University Press, 1962), p. 295.
67. 3.36; Robertson, p. 88.
68. 3.37; Robertson, p. 88.
69. Prol.5; Robertson, p. 4.
70. Prol.6; Robertson, p. 4.
71. See J. Bonnefoy, "Le docteur chrétien selon St. Augustine," *Revue des Etudes Théologiques* 13(1953)25-54.
72. 1.27-30; Robertson, pp. 14-15.
73. *De inv.* 1.8.10, 2.4.12.
74. On this point see, above all, Cicero's discussion of the origins of a worthy rhetoric in *De inventione* 1.

Chapter 4. *Rhetorical Anxiety in Troubadour Lyric*

1. J. Mazzeo, "St. Augustine's Rhetoric of Silence," *Journal of the History of Ideas* 23(1962)175-96.
2. So R. Nouilhat, *Le spiritualisme chrétien dans sa constitution: Approche matérialiste des discours d'Augustin* (Paris: Desclée, 1976); M. Colish, "The Rhetoric of Silence Revisited," *AugStud* 9(1978)15-24; R. Flores, *The Rhetoric of Doubtful Authority* (Ithaca: Cornell University Press, 1984).
3. G. A. Bond has just completed an in-depth study of possible connections between the troubadours and the Loire School of Latin poets. *Traditio*, forthcoming.
4. J. M. Ferrante, "Was Vernacular Poetic Practice a Response to Latin Language Theory?" *Romance Philology* 35(1982)586-600. See also P. Zumthor, *Langue et techniques poétiques à l'époque romaine (XIe-XIIIe siècles)* (Paris: Klincksieck, 1963), who argues that rhetorical taste and expression were filtered between the ninth and eleventh centuries.

Other works on the connection between the Latin system of the liberal arts and Provençal poetry include L. M. Paterson, *Troubadours and Eloquence* (Oxford: Clarendon, 1975), although she shies away from establishing a link between the two and focuses more on the rhetorical concepts developed solely by the troubadours, such as *trobar clus* and *trobar leu.*

5. S. G. Nichols, Jr., "The Promise of Performance: Discourse and Desire in Early Troubadour Lyric," in *The Dialectic of Discovery: Essays on Teaching and Interpretation of Literature Presented to Lawrence E. Harvey*, ed. J. D. Lyons and N. Vickers, French Forum 50 (Lexington, 1984), pp. 93–107.

6. P. Zumthor, "De la circularité du chant (à propos des trouvères des xiie et xiiie siècles)," *Poétique* 2(1970)129-40.

7. On the relation between the troubadour and his audience, see above all F. Goldin, "The Array of Perspectives in the Early Courtly Love Lyric," in *In Pursuit of Perfection*, ed. J. M. Ferrante and G. Economou (New York: Kennikat, 1975), pp. 51-99. See also S. G. Nichols, Jr., "The Medieval Lyric and Its Public," *Mediaevalia et Humanistica* 3(1972)133-53.

8. C. Gross, "Twelfth-Century Views of Time: Philosophic Concepts and Poetic Structures" (diss., Columbia University, 1984).

9. *The Mirror of Narcissus in the Courtly Love Lyric* (Ithaca: Cornell University Press, 1967), pp. 207ff. See also L. Spitzer, *L'amour lointain de Jaufré Rudel et le sens de la poésie des troubadours*, University of North Carolina Studies in Romance Languages and Literatures, 5 (Chapel Hill: University of North Carolina Press, 1944); E. Vance, "Love's Concordance: The Poetics of Desire and the Joy of the Text," *Diacritics* 5(1975)40-52.

10. G. Wolf and R. Rosenstein, eds. and trans., *The Poetry of Cercamon and Jaufré Rudel* (New York: Garland, 1983), no. 6, lines 1-7.

11. Line 12: "ai! car me fos lai pelleris, / si que mos fustz e mos tapis / fos pels sieus bels oills remiratz!" ("Ah! how I wish I were a pilgrim there, / So that my staff and my cloak / Might be seen by her beautiful eyes!").

12. See above, pp. 95–101.

13. Here I would have to disagree with J. Freccero, "Dante's Medusa," in *By Things Seen*, ed. D. L. Jeffrey (Ottawa: University of Ottawa Press, 1979), pp. 33-46, who says, "Ever since Augustine, the Middle Ages insisted upon the link between Eros and language, between the reaching out in desire for what mortals can never possess and the reaching out of language toward the significance of silence. . . . The subject matter of love poetry is poetry, as much as it is love, and the reification of love is at the same time a reification of the words that celebrate passion" (p. 43).

14. So, for example, "Quan lo rius de la fontana," Wolf and Rosenstein, no. 4.

15. See G. A. Bond, ed., *William* vii, Count of Poitiers (New York: Garland, 1982), no. 8, line 26.

16. Bond, no. 9.

17. S. Jaffe, "Antiquity and Innovation in Notker's *Nova rhetorica*: The Doctrine of Invention," *Rhetorica* 3(1985)165-81.

18. P. Piper, ed., *Die Schriften Notkers und seiner Schule*, (Freiburg im Breisgau and Tübingen, 1882), vol. 1, pp. 682-83.

19. Notker tells his readers that they should not make gestures that are too soft ("Nec molliter agitandi sunt gestus") nor should they sway in too womanly a fashion ("nec muliebriter deducenda sunt latera") nor arch their necks too much ("nec iactanda deformiter cervix") (Piper, pp. 682–83).

20. Piper, p. 643. Translation is mine.

21. Bond, no. 4.

22. For a concise survey of scholarship on this poem up to 1967, see L. T. Topsfield, "The Burlesque Poetry of Guilhem IX of Aquitaine," *Neophilologische Mitteilungen* 69(1968)280-302.

23. E. Köhler, "No sai qui s'es—No sai que s'es: Wilhelm IX von Poitiers und Raimbaut von Orange," in his *Esprit und arkadische Freiheit: Aufsätze aus der Welt der Romania* (Frankfurt/Bonn: 1966), pp. 46-66, rpt. in *Mélanges. . .Delbouille* (Gembloux: Duculot, 1964), vol. 2, pp. 349–66. See also J.-C. Payen, *Le Prince d'Aquitaine: Essai sur Guillaume IX, son oeuvre et son érotique* (Paris: Champion, 1980), pp. 85ff, and his article "L'invention idéologique chez Guillaume d'Aquitaine," *Esprit Créateur* 19(1979)95-106. See also M. Stanesco, "L'expérience poétique du 'pur néant' chez Guillaume IX d'Aquitaine," *Médiévales* 6(1984)48-68.

24. L. Lawner, "Notes toward an Interpretation of the *vers de dreyt nien*," *Cultura Neolatina* 28(1968)147-64, p. 155. Also in this camp is N. Pasero, both in his edition of the poet's works, Guglielmo IX d'Aquitania, *Poesie* (Modena: Mucchi, 1973), and in his article "'Devinalh,' 'non-senso,' e 'interiorizzazione testuale,'" *Cultura Neolatina* 28(1968)113-46.

25. As C. Gross ("Twelfth-Century Views of Time") points out, the earliest Chartrian treatises that deal explicitly with the issues of *ex nihilo* creation do not appear until the second decade of the twelfth century. Direct influence is thus not so much the issue here as is Guilhem's "familiarity with the major philosophic issues of his day" (p. 263). See also L. T. Topsfield, *Troubadours and Love* (Cambridge: Cambridge University Press, 1975), p. 263.

26. On the issue of twelfth-century creation theory see W. Wetherbee, *Platonism and Poetry in the Twelfth Century: The Literary Influence of the School of Chartres* (Princeton: Princeton University Press, 1972); F. J. E. Raby, "Nuda Natura and Twelfth-Century Cosmology," *Speculum* 43(1968)72-77; and R. W. Hanning, "Divine Creation and Human Creativity in the Twelfth Century," in *Word, Picture, Spectacle*, ed. Clifford Davidson (Kalamazoo, Mich.: Medieval Institute Publications, 1984), pp. 95-149.

27. J. M. Parent, *La doctrine de la création dans l'Ecole de Chartres* (Paris: Vrin, 1938), p. 131. Translation is mine.

28. In "Norman ni Frances" (*Cultura Neolatina* 30[1970]224-32), L. Lawner argues that this last line of the strophe attacks the humanist poet-clerks of the School of Loire, known for their love poetry "of

Platonic inspiration." Reto Bezzola, *Les origines et la formation de la littérature courtoise en Occident, 500–1200* (Paris: Champion, 1958), claims it is a reflection of the School of Chartres. Either way, these readers support my interpretation.

29. W. T. Pattison, ed., *The Life and Works of the Troubadour Raimbaut d'Orange* (Minneapolis: University of Minnesota Press, 1952), no. 24. Translations are from this edition.

30. For a discussion of these two lyrics in the context of the early troubadour corpus as a whole see J. M. Ferrante, *"Farai un vers de dreyt nien*: The Craft of the Early Trobadors," in *Vernacular Poetics in the Middle Ages*, ed. L. Ebin (Kalamazoo, Mich.: Medieval Institute Publications, 1984), pp. 93-128.

31. W. T. H. Jackson, "Persona and Audience in Two Medieval Love-Lyrics," *Mosaic* 8(1975)147-59.

32. Pattison, no. 39, lines 1-8.

33. Guilhem IX, "Mout jauzens me prenc en amar"; Bond, no. 9, lines 33-36.

34. See Nichols, "The Medieval Lyric and Its Public."

35. Text and translation from the edition by S. G. Nichols, Jr., J. A. Galm, et al., *The Songs of Bernart de Ventadorn*, University of North Carolina Studies in the Romance Languages and Literatures, 39 (Chapel Hill: University of North Carolina Press, 1962), no. 15, lines 1-4.

36. Text and translation from Frederick Goldin, *Lyrics of the Troubadours and Trouvères* (Garden City, N.Y.: Anchor, 1973), p. 193.

37. Works on the *alba* include, above all, J. Saville, *The Medieval Erotic Alba* (New York: Columbia University Press, 1972).

38. S. Spence, "Et Ades Sera l'Alba: *Revelations* as Intertext for the Provençal *Alba*," *Romance Philology* 35(1981)212-17.

39. The best example of this shift is in the *alba* "Reis Glorios" of Giraut de Borneil.

40. So M. Shapiro, "The Figure of the Watchman in the Provençal Erotic Alba," *MLN* 91(1976)607-39.

41. On the rhetorical basis for division of troubadour lyric into its various subgenres see my dissertation, "A Rhetorical Model for the Subgeneric Division of Provençal Lyric" (Columbia University, 1981).

INDEX

A

Abelard, Peter, 116
Adlocutio topos, 92
Aeneas, 49, 50, 57–58; and
  Augustine, 57, 58; and Dido, 30,
  31, 135 n. 12, 36, 41, 45, 46, 57;
  and Icarus, 37, 38, 40–42, 49,
  57–58, 136 n. 25, 139 n. 5; and
  Juno, 23, 24, 25, 48; as orator, 6,
  7, 12, 19, 20, 26; and Theseus,
  136 n. 24; and Turnus, 26,
  37–38, 41, 42, 48, 49, 57, 136 n.
  26, 137 n. 27, 137 n. 28
Alba, 124–25, 151 n. 37, 151 n. 38,
  151 n. 39, 151 n. 40
Allard, G. H., 147 n. 56
Allard, J. B., 145 n. 42
Ambrose, Saint, 64
Amerasinghe, C. W., 134 n. 4
Amor de lonh, in troubadour
  poetry, 109, 149 n. 14
Anderson, W. S., 134 n. 3, 136 n.
  26, 137 n. 27
Annunciation, 86; as model of
  Christian communication, 94,
  104; and the Fall, 77, 80–84, 104;
  medieval depictions of, 87–88

Apollonius of Rhodes, 57
Aristotle: cosmology, 16–18;
  Poetics, 27, 28
Armstrong, A. H., 145 n. 44
Arrigoni, G., 138 n. 33
Audience: and epic, 129;
  participation of, 7, 62, 65, 73, 80,
  82–83, 84, 101, 104, 129; and
  rhetoric, 5, 6, 7, 14, 22; speaker's
  relation to, 40, 76, 122, 129; in
  troubadour lyric, 129, 130
Auerbach, E., 138 n. 33
Augustine, Saint: and catacomb
  paintings, 72, 73; and Cicero,
  139–40 n. 7; *Confessions,* 6,
  55–60, 77–87, 128–29, 129–30,
  139 n. 6; conversation with his
  mother at Ostia, 85–86;
  conversion, 78–85; and creation,
  116; *De catechizandis rudibus,*
  88–89; *De doctrina christiana,*
  94–102, 104, 109, 139 n. 6, 139
  n. 7, 145 n. 45, 147 n. 56, 147 n.
  58, 147–48 n. 59; *De magistro,* 76,
  88, 143–44 n. 26; and erotic
  literature, 106; and language, 76;
  metaphoricity in works of,
  87–90; and pear tree, 77–78; and

Augustine, Saint (*cont.*)
  Platonism, 145 n. 44, 145 n. 45,
    145–46 n. 46; rhetoric in, 6, 7–8,
    103–6, 109, 128–30, 143 n. 24,
    143–44 n. 26, 147 n. 54; sexual
    assumptions, 110–11; theory of
    knowledge, 146 n. 47; and the
    troubadours, 106–27; and Vergil,
    55–60, 85–86, 139 n. 2, 139 n. 5
Augustus, 22–23, 24, 142–43 n. 23
Austin, R. G., 138 n. 38

B

Baker, P. H., 143 n. 26
Balance: in Augustinian and
    Christian rhetoric, 6, 7, 114, 128,
    129; in Vergil, 35, 49
Baldwin, C. S., 140 n. 7
Barilli, R., 132 n. 9
Bassi, D., 139 n. 2
Bernart de Ventadorn, 122, 126
Bezzola, Reto, 151 n. 28
Boethius, 116
Bond, Gerald, 115, 148 n. 3, 149 n.
    15
Bonnefoy, J., 148 n. 71
Bourguet, P. du, 141 n. 11
Bourke, V. J., 146 n. 47
Bovini, G., 141 n. 11
Boyer, C., 146 n. 47
Brakman, C., 138 n. 38
Brandenburg, H., 141 n. 10
Brilliant, R., 146 n. 50
Brown, N., 138 n. 36
Brown, Peter, 139 n. 6
Bubacz, B. S., 146 n. 47
Burke, K., 144 n. 29
Burke, P. F., 137 n. 31

C

Cameron, A., 143 n. 23
Camilla, 21, 38, 43–47, 49, 50, 57,
    137 n. 29, 138 n. 33
Canso, 122, 123–24, 126
Carcopino, J., 138 n. 39
Carletti, C., 142 n. 22
Catacombs, paintings in, 5–6,
    60–73, 80–82, 84, 90–94, 140 n.
    8, 140–41 n. 10, 141 n. 11, 141 n.
    13
Catullus, 142 n. 23
Cavallera, F., 147 n. 58
Charity: Augustine's definition of,
    97; hermeneutics of, 100, 101,
    103, 105–6, 125; and rhetoric,
    148 n. 64; in troubadour lyric,
    123
Chartres, School of, 116, 150 n. 25,
    151 n. 28
Cherchi, P., 140 n. 7
Christ: in the *alba,* 125; as healer,
    99; incarnation of, 96–97
Christianity: evolution of, 8;
    persuasive style, 73–94; and
    rhetoric, 5–6, 7, 8, 94–102,
    104–6, 114
Cicero: and Augustine, 139–40 n. 7;
    changing views on rhetoric,
    131–32 n. 8, 147 n. 54; *De
    inventione,* 13, 14–16, 19, 21, 27,
    34, 78, 95, 100–101, 147 n. 57,
    148 n. 74; *De oratore,* 14, 147 n.
    54; emotion in, 31, 32, 34, 78;
    persuasion in, 76, 79; rhetoric in,
    60, 64, 132 n. 9, 136 n. 17;
    rhetoric and morality in, 13,
    14–16, 18, 19, 20, 46; structure of
    speech in, 131 n. 6; suppression
    in, 29, 34, 80, 101; and the
    troubadours, 112; view of
    audience in, 22, 92, 122
Clarke, M. L., 132 n. 9, 133 n. 24
Clausen, W., 133 n. 1
Clement of Alexandria, 70–71, 93,
    142 n. 21
Coemeterium Maius, 62, 63f, 73, 75
Coffin, H. C., 139 n. 2
Colish, Marcia, 80, 144 n. 35, 144
    n. 36, 148 n. 2
Collard, C., 136 n. 18, 139 n. 4
Commager, Steele, 133 n. 1
Communication: Christian, 90, 93,
    94
Considine, P., 135 n. 12
Constantine, 142–43 n. 23
Control: in rhetoric, 35, 114; and

Control (*cont.*)
the troubadours, 115, 117–18,
119–20, 121–22, 124–27, 129, 130
Cooper, J. C., 144 n. 35
Courcelle, P., 138 n. 39, 139 n. 2,
144 n. 33
Creation, issue of, 40, 116, 150 n.
25, 150 n. 26
Culture: and rhetoric, 1–2, 59
Cupidity: in Christian rhetoric, 97,
104; rhetoric of, 19–20; in Vergil,
47
Currie, H. M., 135 n. 12
Curtius, E. R., 121

D

Daedalus, 37, 38–40, 41, 58, 139 n.
5
Dagens, C., 142 n. 18
D'Ales, A., 145 n. 41
Daly, L. J., 144 n. 33
Daniel, Book of, 72–73
Daniels, D. E., 147 n. 56
Daniels, E. D., 137 n. 28
Dante, 130, 137 n. 29
De Bruyne, L., 141 n. 10, 141 n.
13
Degraff, T. B., 136 n. 15
Della Corte, F., 134 n. 3
Desire: in Augustine, 103, 111; in
classical tradition, 19–21, 22–51,
34; denial of, 2, 5, 6; and reason,
128; and rhetoric, 1–2, 6, 21, 103;
in troubadour poetry, 109, 110,
112, 113–14, 114, 126, 129
Desmouliez, A., 133 n. 20
DeWitt, N.-W., 136 n. 14, 138 n.
33
Dialogue: in the Annunciation, 80,
83; in Augustine, 79, 114
Di Cesare, M. A., 137 n. 27, 138
n. 37
Dido, 21, 29, 30–32, 34–37, 40, 41,
46, 135 n. 11, 135 n. 12, 135 n.
13, 136 n. 14, 136 n. 15, 138 n.
33; and Augustine, 57, 58, 59
Dimock, G. E., 137 n. 27
Divine spark, 89–90, 94, 105, 109,

111, 114, 127, 146 n. 46; legacy
of, 128–30
du Bois, P., 135 n. 12
Duval, Y.-M., 143 n. 23

E

Epic, Vergil's choice of, 129
Essen, C. C. van, 134 n. 10
Evans, V. B., 135 n. 12
Eve, 77, 78, 79, 80, 82–84

F

Faggi, A., 145 n. 40
Faider, P., 138 n. 33
Faith, and rhetoric, 65
Falion, G. M., 134 n. 10
Fall, 77, 79, 83–84
Farron, S. G., 135 n. 12
Ferguson, M. W., 147 n. 56
Ferrante, Joan M., 106, 148 n. 4,
151 n. 30
Ferrari, L. C., 144 n. 27, 144 n. 33
Ferrua, A., 146 n. 48
Fink, J., 146 n. 48
Finney, P. Corby, 142 n. 20
Flores, R., 143 n. 24, 144 n. 33,
148 n. 2
Florus, P. Annius, 133 n. 24
Flotteron, A., 137 n. 30
Fontaine, J., 143 n. 23
Fortin, E. L., 140 n. 7
Freccero, J., 149 n. 13
Frustration, in troubadour poetry,
109, 127, 130
Fuhrmann, M., 143 n. 23

G

Garcia Jimenez, J., 140 n. 7
Garcia Montano, G., 148 n. 64
Garstang, J. B., 137 n. 27
Gassiot-Talabot, G., 140 n. 10
Genovese, E. N., 137 n. 28
Giraut de Borneil, 123–24, 151 n.
39
Goldin, Frederick, 108, 149 n. 7

Grabar, A., 62, 141 n. 11, 141 n. 12
Grabowski, S., 146 n. 47
Gransden K., 137 n. 26
Grant, P., 139 n. 6
Gross, C., 149 n. 8, 150 n. 25
Guilhem IX, 106, 109–10, 114, 115, 117–18, 119, 121, 122, 150 n. 25
Guillaume of Conches, 116

H

Hagendahl, H., 139 n. 2
Hahn, E. A., 134 n. 5, 137 n. 29
Hamilton, W., 145 n. 45
Hanning, R. W., 150 n. 26
Hermeneutics of charity, 100, 101, 103, 105–6, 125
Hierarchy: Christian, 82, 86; humanist, 20–21; inferior elements in, 25–26; in rhetoric, 2, 7, 35; in troubadour poetry, 122
Highbarger, E. L., 136 n. 26
Highet, Gilbert, 20, 133 n. 24, 133 n. 2
Hilary, Saint, 64
Homer, 23, 134
Hoogewerf, G. J., 141 n. 11
Howie, G., 146 n. 47
Huby, J., 145 n. 40
Hugo von Sitten, Bishop, 112
Humanism, 133 n. 18; hierarchy in, 20–21; rhetoric in, 6, 8, 17, 18, 34, 104; and troubadours, 112
Hunt, J. W., 134 n. 3

I

Icarus, 37, 38, 39, 40–41, 49, 50, 57–58, 139 n. 5; and Augustine, 58
Incarnation: of Christ, 96–97; and understanding, 86, 87, 90, 105, 108, 110
Instinct: in Augustine, 7; and persuasion, 34; in Vergil, 30
Irenaeus, 142 n. 20
Isocrates, 5; rhetoric in, 12–13, 14, 18, 20
Iturgaiz, D., 142 n. 20

J

Jackson, B. D., 147 n. 56
Jackson, W. T. H., 119
Jaffe, Samuel, 112
Jansen, F., 140 n. 7
Jaufre Rudel, 108–9
Jerome, Saint, 60–61, 142 n. 16
Johnson, W. R., 22–23, 24, 131 n. 8, 133 n. 1, 134 n. 3, 135 n. 10, 136 n. 26, 137 n. 27
Jolivet, R., 145 n. 44
Joyce, H., 141 n. 10
Juno, 11, 19–20, 21, 22–51, 55–56, 82, 126, 134 n. 3, 134 n. 4
Jupiter, 12, 36, 45, 50
Justin Martyr, 142 n. 16

K

Kalke, C. M., 131 n. 2
Kelley, L. G., 147 n. 56
Kennedy, George A., 2, 13, 132 n. 14, 134 n. 2
Kevane, E., 139 n. 6, 147 n. 52
Kirsch, G. P., 141 n. 11
Kirschbaum, E., 142 n. 20, 146 n. 48
Kitzinger, E., 141 n. 13
Knox, Bernard, 136 n. 19
Köhler, E., 115, 150 n. 23
Kopperschmidt, J., 140 n. 7
Kötzsche-Breitenbruch, L., 146 n. 48
Kristeva, Julia, 7
Kurfess, A., 138 n. 39

L

Lactantius, 64
Landers, Olive Richards, *Hand Book for the Modern Girl,* 2–5, 4f, 8
Language: changing role of, 7; civilizing power of, 12–13; and hierarchy, 20–21; labyrinth of, 42; limitations of, in Christian view, 76, 104; and vision, 86
Last Judgment, 124–25

Latin lyrics, 106, 148 n. 3
Laurand, L., 132 n. 9
Lavin, I., 143 n. 23
Lawner, Lynne, 115, 150 n. 24, 150 n. 28
Loire School, 148 n. 3, 150–51 n. 28
Love, order of, 86, 104
Lover, role of, in troubadour poetry, 109
Lubac, H. de, 145 n. 38
Lucas, J., 132 n. 14
Luke, Gospel of: Annunciation in, 80
Lyrics: Latin, 106, 148 n. 3; troubadour, 106, 108, 129

M

MacKay, L. A., 136 n. 26
Mackendrick, P., 132 n. 9
McNew, Louis D., 140 n. 7
Macrobius, 44–45, 133 n. 24
Madec, G., 143 n. 26
Mallard, W., 144 n. 36
Maréchal, J., 145 n. 40
Mariani, U., 140 n. 7
Marrou, H.-I., 139 n. 2, 141 n. 14, 146 n. 47
Martimort, A.-G., 141 n. 11
Marucchi, O., 140 n. 8
Mary, 105; in Annunciation, 80–84; and troubadour lyric, 122–23
Matier, K. O., 132 n. 9
May, J. M., 132 n. 14
Mazzeo, J., 148 n. 1
Medea, 57, 58, 59, 139 n. 5
Mediation, in Vergil, 49, 50
Mercury, 44–45, 46, 49
Metaphoricity, in Augustine, 87, 90, 110
Michel, A., 132 n. 9, 133 n. 20, 140 n. 7
Mimesis, Aristotle's definition, 27, 28
Mohrmann, C., 140 n. 7
Momigliano, A., 143 n. 23
Monti, R. C., 135 n. 12

Morality, and rhetoric, 12–13, 14–16, 18, 126–27
Moses on Mt. Sinai, catacomb painting, 90–94, 91f
Murphy, James J., 140 n. 7
Mystery, and the sublime, 85, 105

N

Nash, R., 145 n. 44, 146 n. 47
Nature, in Vergil, 30
Neo-Platonists, 90
Neptune, 11–12, 19–20, 30, 31, 78
Nestori, A., 141 n. 11
Nichols, S. G., Jr., 149 n. 5, 149 n. 7, 151 n. 35
Notker III (Notker Labeo), 112–14, 150 n. 19
Nouilhat, R., 144 n. 26, 145 n. 38, 148 n. 2

O

O'Brien, W. J., 144 n. 27
O'Connell, R. J., 146 n. 47
Odgers, M.-M., 135 n. 12
O'Donnell, J. J., 139 n. 2
Ogle, M. B., 135 n. 12
Olbrechts-Tyteca, P., 2
O'Meara, J., 139 n. 2, 139 n. 3
Optatian, 142 n. 23
Orans (praying figure), in early Christian art, 64–67, 69–70, 80, 141 n. 14; and troubadour poetry, 108
Oratio, 64
Orator, as protagonist, 59
Order: of charity, 87–88, 104; narrative, 87; and rhetoric, 14, 20–21, tropic, 87
Origen, 90, 142 n. 16
Oròz, J., 140
Ovid: Medea myth in, 57; and troubadour lyric, 106

P

Pagnini, R. Valenti, 132 n. 9
Participation of audience, 73, 80, 82, 84, 101, 111, 129

Pasero, N., 150 n. 24
Passion, in classical hierarchy, 19–21, 32, 46; in Vergil, 30, 41, 42, 47, 50
Paterson, L. M., 149 n. 4
Pateshull, Peter, 115
Patris, S., 137 n. 31
Payen, J.-C., 150 n. 23
Pease, A. S., 135 n. 12
Pepin, J., 145 n. 44
Perelman, Chaim, 2
Performance, and troubadour poetry, 107, 122, 130
Persuasion: Augustinian view of, 6, 7, 88–89, 110; Christian form of, 73–94; classical view of, 7, 16, 18, 34; in rhetoric and prayer, 65; in troubadour poetry, 108
Petrus and Marcellinus, catacomb of, 65–67
Pfister, K., 142 n. 18
Pilgrim: lover as, in troubadour poetry, 109
Pincherle, A., 144 n. 35
Planh, 126
Plato: and divine spark, 88, 89, 93; and erotic literature, 106; rhetoric in, 14, 20
Plotinus, 90
Porphyry, 90
Pöschl, V., 133 n. 1, 136 n. 23, 138 n. 37
Prayer, and rhetoric, 64–65
Press, G., 146 n. 52
Prete, S., 147 n. 52
Pride, in Vergil, 50
Priscilla, catacomb of, 64, 69–72, 71f, 73, 74f, 80–82, 81f
Prometheus myth, 33–34
Pronuntiatio, Notker's definition, 112
Protevangelium of James, 67–69, 142 n. 16
Putnam, M. C. J., 22–23, 24, 37, 133 n. 1, 134 n. 3, 136 n. 22, 137 n. 27, 137 n. 29, 138 n. 38

Q

Quacquarelli, A., 141 n. 13
Quasten, J., 142 n. 16

Quinn, Kenneth, 137 n. 32
Quintilian, 13

R

Raby, F. J. E., 150 n. 26
Raimbaut d'Aurenga, 118–21, 122, 123, 126
Rambaud, M., 132 n. 9
Reason: and Christianity, 104, 105; and desire, 1–2, 5, 6, 128; and hierarchy, 20–21; and rhetoric, 16; in troubadour poetry, 126; in Vergil, 50
Rebert, H. F., 135 n. 11
Rhetoric: Christian, 79, 84–85, 88, 94–102, 103, 104–6, 129; classical, 1, 2, 7, 11–21, 84, 129, 133 n. 18; and control, 103, 114, 117–22; and culture, 1, 12–13, 15–16, 17, 18, 46, 59; and desire, 103, 113–14; and emotion, 31, 34; and faith, 65; and issue of creation, 116–17; as literary theme, 1; and moral integrity, 13–14; opposing type, 19–20, 31, 32; and order, 14, 20–21; and prayer, 64–65; in troubadour poetry, 107–27
Rieck, J., 143 n. 26
Ripanti, G., 147 n. 52
Riskin, Jessica, 136 n. 25
Robertson, D. W., 95, 97
Romeuf, J., 135 n. 10
Rostovtzeff, M. I., 141 n. 10

S

St. Hilaire, G., 145 n. 40
St-Laurent, G. de, 142 n. 14
Schmid, W., 140 n. 7
Schmidt-Dengler, W., 140 n. 7
Schmitz, A., 136 n. 16
Schumacher, W. N., 146 n. 48
Scipioni, L. I., 148 n. 64
Seduction, in rhetoric, 1, 2, 19–20, 21, 112
Sedulius, 142 n. 23
Segal, C., 135 n. 10
Sejourne, P., 144 n. 33
Semple, W. H., 135 n. 12, 137 n. 27, 140 n. 7

Servius, 44
Seventh Letter, 89–90, 110, 111, 114
Shapiro, M., 151 n. 40
Silence, in Augustinian rhetoric, 7, 104
Simon, M., 146 n. 48
Sirventes, 126
Smirin, V. M., 134 n. 2
Solodow, J., 133 n. 21
Speech, structure of, in Cicero, 131 n. 6
Spence, S., 151 n. 38, 151 n. 41
Spitzer, L., 109, 149 n. 9
Springer, L. A., 131 n. 7, 134 n. 2
Stahl, H. P., 137 n. 27
Stanesco, M., 150 n. 23
Stevenson, J., 140 n. 8
Stuiber, A., 142 n. 20
Suchocki, M., 145 n. 41
Suppression, in humanist rhetoric, 2, 6, 29, 34, 35, 59, 80, 82, 101

T

Testini, P., 140 n. 8
Theseus, 139 n. 3, 139 n. 5
Thom, S., 135 n. 12
Thornton, A. H. F., 136 n. 26, 137 n. 27
Topsfield, L. T., 150 n. 22, 150 n. 25
Troilus, 29, 30, 35, 37, 47, 135 n. 11
Tronzo, W., 140 n. 8, 146 n. 48
Troubadours: and Augustine, 106–27; rhetoric of, 6–7, 8, 107–27, 128, 129
Turnus, 21, 26, 37–38, 42–43, 47–49, 57, 134 n. 3, 137 n. 28, 137 n. 29

V

Vaccari, A., 138 n. 39

Vance, Eugene, 85, 131 n. 2, 139 n. 6, 144 n. 35, 145 n. 39, 149 n. 9
Van der Meer, F., 144 n. 29, 145 n. 41
Van Nortwick, T., 136 n. 26
Venus, in Vergil, 31, 85
Vergil: *Aeneid,* 11–51, 128, 142 n. 23; antirhetorical elements in, 20, 108; and Augustine, 55–60, 85–86, 139 n. 2, 139 n. 5; and Cicero, 131 n. 7; desire in, 22–51; fourth Eclogue, 51, 138 n. 38, 138 n. 39; and Jerome, 61; rhetoric in, 6, 7, 11–21, 106, 133 n. 24
Verheijen, L. M. J., 146 n. 52
Via Latina catacomb, 90, 91f
Visual imagery, and Christianity, 86, 90, 110
Vitruvius, 27–28, 32–34, 46
Vries, S. F. de, 135 n. 12

W

Walter, F., 140 n. 7
Watchman, in troubadour *alba,* 125–26
West, D., 137 n. 26
West, G. S., 137 n. 30, 138 n. 33
Wetherbee, W., 150 n. 26
Will: in Augustine, 79, 111; and the troubadours, 129
Williams, R. D., 134 n. 10
Women: in Augustine, 111; in troubadour lyric, 111–16, 121–23; in Vergil, 43, 47, 137 n. 30

Z

Zangara, V., 145 n. 40
Zumthor, P., 148 n. 4, 149 n. 6

Library of Congress Cataloging-in-Publication Data

Spence, Sarah, 1954–
    Rhetorics of reason and desire : Vergil, Augustine, and the
troubadours / Sarah Spence.
        p.   cm.
    Bibliography: p.
    ISBN 0-8014-2129-2
    1. Virgil. Aeneis.   2. Virgil—Influence.   3. Aeneas (Legendary
character) in literature.   4. Rhetoric, Ancient, in literature.
5. Desire in literature.   6. Augustine, Saint, Bishop of Hippo—
Views on rhetoric.   7. Troubadours.   8. Provençal poetry—History
and criticism.   9. Rhetoric, Medieval, in literature.   I. Title.
PA6825.S64 1988
873'.01—dc19   87-47953

2003. 07. 22 B   41.95 (4.98)